street smart
sustainability

THE SOCIAL VENTURE NETWORK SERIES

street smart sustainability

**THE ENTREPRENEUR'S GUIDE
TO PROFITABLY GREENING
YOUR ORGANIZATION'S DNA**

David Mager

Joe Sibilia

BK

Berrett–Koehler Publishers, Inc.
San Francisco
a BK Business book

Berrett-Koehler Publishers, Inc.
235 Montgomery Street, Suite 650
San Francisco, CA 94104-2916
Tel: (415) 288-0260   Fax: (415) 362-2512   www.bkconnection.com

Ordering Information

Quantity sales. Special discounts are available on quantity purchases by corporations, associations, and others. For details, contact the "Special Sales Department" at the Berrett-Koehler address above.

Individual sales. Berrett-Koehler publications are available through most bookstores. They can also be ordered directly from Berrett-Koehler: Tel: (800) 929-2929; Fax: (802) 864-7626; www.bkconnection.com

Orders for college textbook/course adoption use. Please contact Berrett-Koehler: Tel: (800) 929-2929; Fax: (802) 864-7626.

Orders by U.S. trade bookstores and wholesalers. Please contact Ingram Publisher Services, Tel: (800) 509-4887; Fax: (800) 838-1149; E-mail: customer.service@ ingrampublisherservices.com; or visit www.ingrampublisherservices.com/Ordering for details about electronic ordering.

Berrett-Koehler and the BK logo are registered trademarks of Berrett-Koehler Publishers, Inc.

Printed in the United States of America

Berrett-Koehler books are printed on long-lasting acid-free paper. When it is available, we choose paper that has been manufactured by environmentally responsible processes. These may include using trees grown in sustainable forests, incorporating recycled paper, minimizing chlorine in bleaching, or recycling the energy produced at the paper mill.

Library of Congress Cataloging-in-Publication Data
Mager, David.
  Street smart sustainability : the entrepreneur's guide to profitably greening your organization's DNA / David Mager, Joe Sibilia.
    p. cm. (The social venture network series)
  Includes bibliographical references and index.
  ISBN 978-1-60509-465-6 (pbk. : alk. paper)
  1. Business enterprises—Environmental aspects. 2. Entrepreneurship—Environmental aspects. 3. Social responsibility of business. 4. Sustainability. I. Sibilia, Joe. II. Title.
  HD30.255.M327   2010
  658.4'083—dc22   2010034781

FIRST EDITION
15 14 13 12 11 10   10 9 8 7 6 5 4 3 2 1

Cover design by Crowfoot/Leslie Waltzer
Cover photo by Roxanne Crocker
Book design and production by Bev Butterfield, Girl of the West Productions
Copyediting by PeopleSpeak
Indexing by Rachel Rice

*This book is dedicated to the Goddess whom we serve
and the many forms she takes, including that of
our wives and daughters: Deborah, Rachelle, Roxanne,
and Sadie and Claire, Kristen, Kendra, and Kayla*

Contents

Letter from the Editor of the Social Venture Network Series

These days, every Tom, Dick, and Harry in business wants to be "Green"—and half of them claim they are, usually with little or no basis in reality.

But what can you do if you *want* to walk the talk of sustainability? How can you transform your business to ensure that your environmental footprint is as small as it can feasibly be and your workplace, your employees, and your community are as safe as possible from threats to human health and the environment? And if you're just starting a business, what practical steps can you take right now to put your company on the path to sustainability?

Street Smart Sustainability was written for you.

If you own, manage, or work in a small or medium-sized business—or, for that matter, a nonprofit organization or government agency—or if you're planning a new venture, David Mager and Joe Sibilia's brilliant little handbook is the essential tool to understand and implement the principles of sustainability from a practical perspective. Between the covers of this remarkably thin volume you'll find detailed, in-depth advice about how to conceive, plan, and implement steps to conserve energy, water, the raw materials in your products, and other resources; lower your carbon output; curtail or divert waste—and to measure your progress with precise, scientifically grounded methods. *Street Smart Sustainability* will help you manage your facilities and your employees alike in ways that will boost productivity, reduce your impact on the environment, and make more money. And just because I've mentioned money last, don't think it's an afterthought in this book:

the time-tested premise of *Street Smart Sustainability* is that the sustainable course is almost always the more profitable one.

Given David Mager's deep grounding in science and technology, the book's emphasis on measurement and precision, and both authors' nearly lifelong experience in promoting sustainability in business, you might expect this book to be full of mysterious jargon and to be virtually unreadable as a result. But that's not so, I'm happy to report! *Street Smart Sustainability* is written in plain, everyday English, and it's chock full of engaging anecdotes as reported by the founders and CEOs of real businesses who have taken steps to green their own operations. This is a practical handbook. It was written for *you*.

If you want to increase the sustainability of your company, you have three broad options:

1. Retain a specialized consultant to assess your company's operations and recommend a course of action for you to follow.

2. Rely on word-of-mouth from employees, friends, and owners or managers of similar businesses.

3. Read *Street Smart Sustainability*—and then purchase extra copies to distribute to your managers or even all your employees.

Of these three options, the safest—and by far the cheapest in the long run—is number 3. Even if you decide to pursue the first or the second of the three, you'll save yourself a lot of money, a great deal of time, and much grief if you first read *Street Smart Sustainability*, anyway.

After all, isn't reading a little book the least you can do to save the planet?

MAL WARWICK
Berkeley, California
October 2010

Acknowledgments

From David

I want to acknowledge my parents, Gerard and Muriel, who always made me feel like there were no limits to what I could do. To my beautiful wife, Deborah, and daughters, Rachelle, Roxanne, and Sadie, who taught me and keep teaching me what it is to be a human being. To my sisters, Hillary and Cindy, for their love and their artistic and graphic designs. To my stepsons, Brendan and Isaiah. I want to thank all of my comrades at Students for Environmental Action who worked with me in the 1960s every day after school at 80 Central Park West in building the environmental movement. At the time we thought we were changing the world—and we did. They are Lorna Nowve, Paul Geffner, Peter Arno, Lewis Clayton, Evan Giller, Roger Gutentag, Mark Schweitzer, Hillary Mager, Vicki and Mark Judson, and Steve Nadel. To my science teachers who took me out of the classroom and put me to work in the school labs—Tony Carr at Robert Hutchings Goddard Junior High School and Arnold Bellush, Grace Tilger, and Mildred Sickles at Stuyvesant High School. To my professors who helped me decide to not go into medicine but to do pioneering work in the new fields of renewable energy and environmental sciences—Dr. Douglas J. Futuyma, Distinguished Professor of Ecology and Evolution, and Dean John G. Truxal, Distinguished Teaching Professor of Technology and Society, both at State University of New York at Stony Brook; Professor Peter Woodhead, director of the Discovery Bay Marine Laboratory, and William E. Heronemus, professor of civil engineering at University of

Massachusetts, with whom I share two patents; and my late friend Dr. Isaac Asimov, who served on the board of my first company and helped promote my ocean thermal energy conversion and mariculture inventions.

To all my clients who let me come into their companies, allowed me to discover their secrets, and played with me as we explored how to get rich at being greener. To Rena Shulsky-David, who was my most significant mentor in the environmental arena and in helping me find my spiritual path. To my rabbis Sheila Weinberg and Efraim Eisen. To my other "rabbis," Zenmaster Roshi Bernie Glassman, Venerable Gyoway Kato, Venerable Sister Clare Carter, and Prakash Laufer. To my great business mentors, Jack Dushey, Jack Grumet, and Mike Walsh. To my metateachers in the green space—Denis Hayes and Terry Gips. To my core team of sustainability expert partners, Valerie Douglas, Don Stone, Eduardo Suarez, and the late Kitty Gillespie. To my shrink, John Dolven. To the men in my weekly 5 a.m. Amen Spiritual Warriors' men's group who helped raise me these last fifteen years, Vijay Bickford, Adam Bauer, Paul Bourke, Henry Eberhardt, George Levinger, Dennis Rosen, Peter McAvoy, Steven Cronen-Townsend, Harvey Rivard, and Joe Laur; my sponsors in doing men's work, Paul Weinberg and Sam Rodgers; and my teacher, Justin Sterling.

Mostly, I want to acknowledge Joe Sibilia for being my friend these last fifteen years, for finding cool things for me to do in the sustainability arena, and for his partnership in creating this book. More than anyone I know, Joe sees the special gifts and deep beauty in everyone he meets.

From Joe

Since this is primarily a business book, in contrast to a philosophical book, my acknowledgments will focus on the "education of a street kid turned social entrepreneur." As part of my education, I would like to thank my mom for forcing me to attend summer school and learn the English language. I'm still learning. Since my primary place of stay was not with my dad, I learned the fine arts of business under his tutelage, outside the home. He teaches me daily.

To my grandmother Angelina Fiorentino and Aunt Antoinette, who taught me the faith in prayer and understanding for those with physical challenges.

Father George Concordia, a Dominican priest, exemplified the dignity of a spiritual life, while pursuing the arts of business, for the benefit of his church. I learned the value of values-driven investment research. He was also my philosophy professor.

Three lawyers taught me the value of the rule of law in a civil society: Frank Sullivan, Charlie Ryan, and Frank Fitzgerald. Frank Fitzgerald exposed me to the world of banking while forming, operating, and selling the Bank of Western Massachusetts. He continues to teach me.

My two accountants, Jay O'Brien and John Turgeon, disciplined me financially. I'm a work in progress.

The Social Venture Network taught me the value of experimenting beyond my comfort zone. Integrating business, community, and spirit gave me new life.

The Corner Fellas (geographically), Bill "Boy" Raschi, Gary "The Hammer" Zaiken, John "Meathead" Rowley, Mark "Markie Marc" Antaya, Mike "Oki" O'Connor, Tom "Fro" Frodema, Brenden "BB, Brad, Bradley" Reilly, the importer of talent and producer "Malibu" Jack Wysocki, Lloyd Vaudrin, "Butch" Peter Paul Pepin, John "Johnny" Bernardi, Bill Kemple, Kevin "The King" Barbeau, and Pete "The Kid" Kenyon, deserve special mention, and I hope to devote an entire book to their street corner lessons.

Our entire CSRwire.com team, led by Jan Morgan, has given me the support to spend time on the book and promote its contents. Thank you for being a "high-tech, high-touch, high-performance" enterprise.

The community of the Gasoline Alley Foundation continues to inspire me, led by Rob Thomas of Social(k) fame, pioneer Eileen Sullivan, Michelle Scibelli, Denise LaBelle, Athan "Soco" Catjakis, John Majeracek, Trent Guihan, Jake Bouchard, Tony Taylor, and everyone else that strives to "give value to that which has been abandoned."

All the detractors, misguided colleagues, pseudofriends, investment bankers, and ill-informed business professionals who still believe business is designed exclusively to make money, without any other consideration, continue to give me the strength to forge ahead. They shall remain nameless.

The support of my extended families and friends lets me know whom I can depend on in times of need: Jerry Gorde, Rich Gallivan, Doug and Anne Stockbridge, Marion and Greg Sullivan, David and Ben Sullivan, Mark and Thelma Sullivan, Jean and Al Easterday, Trudy Sullivan, and all the kids that make my life better by knowing them and hoping we leave them a better place to live.

To John Stossel of Fox News, who has helped me frame our argument by persuasively presenting the other side, and to Congressman Rich Neal, who has demonstrated the value of loyalty.

Finally, to my coauthor, David Mager, who did most of the heavy lifting for the book and continues to strive to become a better man.

From David and Joe

Together, we can't show enough appreciation to Sharon Goldinger, our editor, who worked magic; to Mal Warwick and Deb Nelson, who said yes to this project, and to all of our dear friends at Social Venture Network. We wish to thank Andrew Frothingham, an early editor. We would like to acknowledge the entire crew of Berrett-Koehler and the folks that read and sometimes reread and reviewed this manuscript in its earlier draft, Doug Dupler, Chuck Ehrlich, Josh O'Conner, and Kendra Armer. We also want to acknowledge "Malibu" Jack Wysocki, who came up with the title for this book, and David's daughter Roxanne for the cover photo. We especially want to acknowledge all the entrepreneurs who allowed us to tell their stories in this book.

Introduction

This book is for leaders of small and medium-sized organizations who want to take the steps necessary to achieve environmental sustainability in a practical and cost-effective manner. No business on the planet meets all the criteria of a fully sustainable enterprise. The fundamental challenge for any small to medium-sized organization is determining how much time and money to take away from day-to-day operations and invest in becoming sustainable. But, as you will see from the many examples offered, it makes business and environmental sense to implement as many of the recommendations found in this book as possible—even in challenging economic times.

It has taken forty years since the first Earth Day for sustainability to become an "overnight success." Today, after years of scientific evidence, protest marches, consumer boycotts, growing public demand, successful lawsuits by public interest and environmental groups, increased shareholder value to companies that embrace sustainability, and environmental causes championed by celebrities and thought leaders, the idea of sustainability in business is almost universally accepted.

Recent polls show that 80 percent of the American people are motivated by environmental issues[1] and 95 percent of shoppers are open to green products.[2] The Era of Sustainability has arrived. Centuries of spending the earth's capital as if it were in endless supply and exploiting the environment as if it were one's private profit center have given way to enrolling all stakeholders in environmental decision making. Combining this with the evolution of environmental technology, we are approaching the point where sustainability is an economic driver and a competitive advantage.

Street Smart Sustainability: The Entrepreneur's Guide to Profitably Greening Your Organization's DNA provides the reader with practical best practices to create a sustainable enterprise in a cost-effective manner. We're not merely making the case for sustainability. Our book is designed for those who have already accepted sustainability as an initiative worthy of their time and effort. It provides the leaders of small and medium-sized organizations with simple tools to make continuous, cost-effective improvements in their sustainability practices—practices that diffuse into the organizational DNA and become fixtures, shifting the prevailing corporate culture.

Many how-to books build your skill set from one chapter to the next. By the end of the book you can put the new skills into effect. *Street Smart Sustainability* takes a different approach. Individual chapters are designed to act as stand-alone sets of action steps on particular topics. They can be read and the recommendations implemented sequentially, or they can be read in random or impulse order. The book takes advantage of your intuitive understanding of the principal functions that any organization must engage in, such as facility selection and maintenance, energy and water use, purchasing, and waste disposal. It is supplemented by a Web site that acts as a repository of information on all the topics, searchable by key word, with interactive question-and-answer functionality in a user-generated module. We hope to collaborate with other efforts on the topic to ensure the most comprehensive resource available.

Each chapter provides a series of action steps on a particular initiative and is designed to inspire new business opportunities. For example, your waste can become another enterprise's raw materials and a cost savings could result in an income-generating collaboration. Each chapter also ends with a summary listing some recommended opportunities for cost-effective sustainability.

Most small and medium-sized businesses operate without the luxury of management depth and outside advisors and they need to make progressive changes over a period of time. Read the chapter on purchasing or carbon footprint, and you may implement those recommendations while managing your enterprise in a day-to-day manner. Do everything in all the chapters, and your organization will become much more sustainable. The book also includes tools to allow you to measure progress and savings.

Street Smart Sustainability is designed to be a road map to the sustainable "low-hanging fruit." Following the 80/20 Rule, this short book cannot be a comprehensive guide to sustainability, but it should provide 80 percent of the guidance that a 1,000-page book on the subject would provide. How to make your organization sustainable may seem like too big of a topic to squeeze into a small book, but we, as the authors, have been extremely lucky to have had a medley of life experiences that have greatly helped us tackle such an audacious goal.

While attending Stuyvesant High School in New York in 1968, David got involved with Students for Environmental Action and ultimately ended up being a co-organizer of the first Earth Day in 1970. Since that time he has helped over 300 companies become greener profitably. A pioneer in performing comprehensive sustainability audits, David audited and did other environmental work with a large number of Social Venture Network (SVN) companies, including Stonyfield Farm, Aveda, Tommy Boy Entertainment, Motherwear, Blue Fish Clothing, Mal Warwick Associates, Rhino Records, and Eileen Fisher.

David was also the director of standards of the first U.S. environmental certification and labeling organization, Green Seal, where he oversaw the development of standards for energy-efficient lighting, water-efficient fixtures, recycled paper, rerefined engine oil, household cleaners, paints, appliances, and other consumer products. He also worked with the environmental-standard-setting bodies of other countries to globally harmonize environmental product standards.

He represented the United States and the American National Standards Institute (ANSI) in the creation of the global ISO 14000 standards for environmental management systems. He also worked with the U.S. Environmental Protection Agency (EPA) and other environmental scientists from around the country in the creation of the life cycle analysis (LCA) methodology. David is also a partner in Meadowbrook Lane Capital.

Joe did not wake up one day and say, "I'm going to pursue sustainable business principles and practices." His has been a gradual evolution from street kid to social entrepreneur. Joe started a company with an innovative and environmentally superior way of dispensing fruit juices as fountain drinks. The creation of this technology, as well as new formulas, resulted in the elimination of bottles, cans, packaging, and refrigeration and in 1994 alone saved 50,880 trees, 20,966,400 gallons of water, 9,974 cubic yards of landfill space, 12,579,840 kilowatt-hours (kWh) of energy, and 179,712 pounds of potentially air-polluting effluents. Since then, the technology has positively impacted the environment beyond expectations, and the Pepsi Cola Company has purchased the formulas, technology, and brand for distribution and integration worldwide.

Joe created Meadowbrook Lane Capital, a socially responsible investment bank, which was, as the *Wall Street Journal* described, the "White Knight" in the Ben & Jerry's Unilever transaction, preserving ten of the social and environmental initiatives of Ben & Jerry's.[3] Through Meadowbrook Lane Capital, Joe has bought and sold nineteen businesses. For each successive business he improved his sustainable practices, culminating in the purchase of CSRwire.com as a vehicle to distribute and archive sustainability news and reports, organize the world's sustainability information, and act as an open-source platform for innovative financial instruments and structures to demonstrate that business can be a tool for creating a just and sustainable planet. Joe is also the founder of the Gasoline Alley Foundation, designed to "teach inner city and underprivileged persons to become successful entrepreneurs using socially responsible/sustainable business practices while revitalizing inner city neighborhoods."[4] The foundation has incubated over forty sustainable enterprises.

Both of us have the perspective of seeing firsthand hundreds of sustainability practices done right and done wrong. We have been friends for fifteen years and have collaborated on many ventures for over a decade.

The book uses examples from a large variety of small and medium-sized organizations, most of which we have worked with. Most chapters include a story about Stonyfield Farm or Aveda. Both of these companies now have multihundred million dollars in annual sales, but they both started out as struggling little companies. Their goals were not to become multihundred-million-dollar companies but to heal the planet. Both have become hugely successful not despite their sustainability practices but because of them.

Every organization begins moving toward sustainability by having a visionary leader who decides that sustainability is an important objective of the company. Chapter 1 discusses how the leader gets employee "buy-in" to the vision and guides and motivates the company into becoming sustainable.

Once the leader and employees adopt a vision for sustainability, the next step is to measure where the company currently is, how far it has to go, and what it has to do to realize the vision. A baseline sustainability audit is the first step in measuring your organization's impact on the environment and becomes the basis from which you can monitor and make continuous improvement toward sustainability. Chapter 2 provides a how-to on performing your sustainability audit.

With the sustainability vision articulated and invested in company-wide, and with the audit results tabulated and comprehended, a sustainability plan needs to be developed and implemented. The mechanics of this are described in chapter 3 along with an overview of several very effective, field-proven sustainability management tools, frameworks, and standards—such as the CERES (Coalition of Environmentally Responsible Economies) Principles, the ISO (International Standards Organization) 14000 standards for Environmental Management Systems, and the Natural Step Framework—that are being successfully employed by small and medium-sized enterprises. Chapter 3 explains the differences between these tools and provides guidance on which ones to select.

If you can measure it, you can manage it. In chapter 4, you'll find other very powerful metrics you can use in becoming sustainable. These tools will help you quantify your waste, analyze the entire life cycle of your product or service from cradle to grave, and figure out the economics of your sustainability initiatives.

The most effective way to be green is not to remediate but to design products and services sustainably from the start. Chapter 5 provides simple green design rules.

Chapter 6 discusses the impact of facilities on the environment and outlines the steps necessary to make a greener facility.

The sustainable energy initiative consists of maximizing your energy conservation while maximizing the percent of renewable energy you use. Chapter 7 relays renewable energy options and energy conservation measures while providing instructions on how to conduct your energy audit.

Once you know your total energy use, you can calculate your carbon footprint. Chapter 8 provides the formula for converting your energy use numbers into carbon dioxide (CO_2) emissions and then offers recommendations to mitigate your carbon footprint.

One of the biggest impacts organizations have on the environment is through their purchases. Chapter 9 provides tools for assessing vendors' sustainability practices and how to implement green purchasing.

"Reduce, reuse, recycle" is the mantra for entry-level responsible environmental stewardship. Chapter 10 provides the strategies and tactics to cost-effectively reduce emissions to air, releases to water, and disposal of solid waste.

In nature, there is no such thing as waste. Chapter 11 explains the methods successfully employed by many companies to use waste as a raw material. It also looks at the implications for the planet and on the bottom line, turning an environmental problem into a business opportunity.

Street Smart Sustainability: The Entrepreneur's Guide to Profitably Greening Your Organization's DNA is for entrepreneurs who already agree with the necessity of making their businesses sustainable. However, others—a relative, spouse, employee, lawyer, banker, vendor, customer—may not agree and will ask, "What! Are you nuts? Why are you doing this?" For them we've provided the "Top Ten Sustainability Talking Tips" and data to support what is already in your head, heart, and soul.

Top Ten Sustainability Talking Tips

It makes sense to green your organization's DNA because sustainability

1. Reduces the cost of goods
2. Improves sales and market share
3. Attracts and retains talented employees
4. Improves community relations
5. Prevents arbitrary new regulations
6. Increases access to capital
7. Increases valuation
8. Builds customer loyalty
9. Facilitates partnerships
10. Creates peace of mind

REDUCE THE COST OF GOODS

Companies take their retained earnings and, instead of cashing out at the end of the day, reinvest them into making products or services. Companies make two types of products: intended products, which they sell, and unintended products, which they have to pay to dispose of. The latter is often what adversely impacts the environment. When companies learn to reduce or eliminate their unintended products, they invariably reduce their cost of goods and lower their risks.

For one company in the automotive industry, we worked on reducing the amount of toxic chemicals and harmful solvents purchased and their subsequent disposal. The employees who witnessed these reductions felt better about their relationship with the company. Pride and productivity increased. With fewer chemical purchases, costs were reduced, dumping fees were reduced, and less refuse traveled down the drain to attract the attention of the community.

The plant manager said, "Is this stuff environmental?" and when he was answered with "Yes!" he said, "Let's do more of this stuff."

IMPROVE SALES AND MARKET SHARE

In a 2009 study commissioned by Green Seal and EnviroMedia Social Marketing and conducted by Opinion Research, 82 percent of consumers bought green products despite the battered economy and the fact that in some cases the products cost more. Of the 1,000 people surveyed, 505 bought just as many green products today as they did before the economic downturn, while 19 percent said they bought more and 14 percent bought fewer.[5]

Another survey tool shows that the LOHAS (Lifestyles of Health and Sustainability) population is large and growing. This market segment covers people interested in personal health, green building, eco-tourism, natural lifestyles, alternative transportation, and alternative energy. This group currently represents 41 million American consumers and is worth about $209 billion in consumer (excluding business-to-business) sales.[6] The percent of green buyers is even higher in Europe than in the United States.

Jeffrey Hollender, cofounder of Seventh Generation, insists that his company's success is largely due to being recognized as an innovator of products made from sustainable materials. If you want to position your products or services where money and growth are, sustainability is the place.

ATTRACT AND RETAIN TALENTED EMPLOYEES

A study of 800 MBA students from eleven leading North American and European business schools found that 94 percent of the students would accept a lower salary, an average of 14 percent less, to work for a company with a reputation for being environmentally responsible and for caring about employees and other stakeholders. It also showed that companies that subscribe to socially responsible business practices consistently attract the cream of the crop from the best business schools.[7]

For example, at Harvard Business School, one of the largest and fastest growing clubs is the Social Enterprise Club. Net Impact, an organization founded as Students for Social Responsibility, has grown into a network of 15,000 emerging business leaders in 250 chapters.[8]

Employees love to be on the side of the "good guys." Worker productivity is high in companies that are proactive environmentally.

Imagine the difference it will make to your bottom line to attract great people seeking jobs with your company who will stay with your company for as long as they can and work for you as productively as possible. That is what sustainability can do for you.

IMPROVE COMMUNITY RELATIONS

Poor corporate citizenship attracts the attention of activists ready to hold the company accountable and diminishes the prospect of community support for corporate initiatives that need community support.

With the advent of e-mail and social media tools such as Twitter, YouTube, Facebook, MySpace, and LinkedIn, word gets out quickly and effectively. A simple camera phone can record an environmental indiscretion. The knowledge that a company is seeking to make continuous progress in its sustainability practices addresses many concerns of the community and fosters more cooperative company-community relations.

PREVENT ARBITRARY REGULATIONS

The costs associated with public policy initiatives and regulations that may undermine a company's activities have been well documented. Mitigating these initiatives requires legions of lobbyists, distracts management, and detracts from brand value. However, when a company strives toward sustainability and environmental excellence, and when industry acts in a proactive, environmentally and socially responsible manner, the need for government regulations is reduced as are the costs associated with influencing public policy.

As pointed out by Professor Ronald Coase of the University of Chicago Law School, winner of the 1991 Nobel Prize in Economics, when companies fulfill their "social contract" with consumers, regulations are not needed. Government regulations fill the vacuum created when industry fails to maintain this contract.

In addition, federal regulations established by Office of Management and Budget Circular A-119 state that when an existing voluntary standard works, regulations need not follow, and the voluntary standards can be the basis for government procurement decisions.[9]

Many companies, instead of becoming "victims" of legislation, are being proactive. They are designing products and services that meet present and pending environmental and sustainability standards. In doing so, they reduce the likelihood that new regulations will require increases in product or service costs and management attention. For the small to medium-sized enterprise, government fines and procedural changes can be severely costly.

INCREASE ACCESS TO CAPITAL

The Social Investment Forum reports that in 2007, $2.7 trillion was placed in investments that had social or environmental screens applied to them. As a percent of all assets under management, socially responsible investing grew at a rate of 18 percent over the previous year, compared with a growth of 3 percent for all assets under management.[10]

These investments have been also described as *patient*, indicating a way that allows management to invest with a long-term view in mind. One of the most active organizations for socially screened, private, patient capital is Investors' Circle, whose members have invested $134 million in over 200 deals since 1992.[11] One of the founders of Investors' Circle, Woody Tasch, has been promulgating the notion of "slow money" supporting local living economies for small to medium-sized businesses.

By the way, the Internal Revenue Service is anticipating an enormous transfer of wealth over the next few years. This transfer will create several million new millionaires as parents who lived during the depression and World War II transfer their wealth, through inheritance, to their baby boomer children. Baby boomers have proven to be the most active participants in the sustainability movement.

Do you need capital to grow, to access new markets, or for capital equipment? Several trillion dollars says that investors will give it to you only if you are sustainable and socially or environmentally responsible. What are you waiting for?

INCREASE VALUATION

So, how did all this socially screened investment capital perform? Great. Socially responsible investors are *investors*, not philanthropists giving away their money, and like other investors they seek as high a return on their investment capital as is prudent to expect—at least competitive with other investments. The United Nations (UN) did an analysis of ten key broker studies and twenty influential academic works to explore the link between socially responsible investments (SRIs) and investment performance. The study found that SRIs are competitive with non-SRIs.[12] In addition, 322 other studies showed that SRI mutual fund performance is comparable to non-SRI mutual fund performance.[13] The Domini Index, the oldest SRI index, showed an average annualized return of 8.43 percent though December 2008, compared to 7.78 percent for the S&P 500.[14] (The index was renamed the FTSE KLD 400 Social Index in 2009.)

Many companies illustrate that sustainability creates greater value. Ben & Jerry's grew into a multinational company. Its growth, development, and leadership coincided with the company's experiments in the sustainability movement. During the hostile takeover by Unilever in 2000, Ben & Jerry's retained Meadowbrook Lane Capital to save the social and environmental mission of the company. During that rescue, the stock increased from $17.00 a share to $43.60. By dramatizing the brand value associated with sustainability, we uncovered significant value that Unilever voluntarily agreed to accept.

In other instances familiar to many readers, Stonyfield Farm began as a modest enterprise and was sold to Groupe Danone at a super premium; Tom's of Maine began as a real mom-and-pop enterprise with Tom and Kate Chappell and was sold to Colgate at a super premium; the Body Shop started in a kitchen, went public, and demonstrated super premium value; Odwalla squeezed juice from real fruit and went public, and Coca-Cola ultimately purchased the company at a premium; Joe sold one of his companies to the Pepsi Cola Company at a significant premium; and the modest single restaurant White Dog Cafe was able to require a social contract from its buyer (in which the buyer agreed to many brand value requirements—even the soap used in the kitchen!). Sustainability creates greater value.

BUILD CUSTOMER LOYALTY

Being sustainable—environmentally and socially responsible—turns you into a hero in the eyes of your customers, financiers, partners, peers, friends, and family.

Conversely, decision makers at companies with bad environmental performance are shunned and ostracized in social and familial circles. For example, the tuna boycott was successful not just because of the economic damage to the companies that were boycotted. It was successful because, in one case, a young girl wouldn't sit on the lap of the chairman of one of the largest canned tuna companies "until you stop killing dolphins, Grandpa!" This company stopped killing dolphins.[15]

A revealing article in the *New York Times* disclosed that chromium platers were cleaning up their operations not because regulatory compliance made business unprofitable but because their neighbors wouldn't talk to them anymore. They were socially ostracized at church, on the golf course, and at the bridge table because of their unsustainable practices.[16]

FACILITATE PARTNERSHIPS

Conscious sustainability naturally attracts like-minded people. Collaborating with waste stream partners or supply chain partners, or forming an alliance with a larger company that aspires to connect with sustainability, facilitates partnerships.

For example, an entire business was created on the idea of supplying Ben & Jerry's with brownies made by a bakery operated by people who were living in poverty. Better World Books takes used and outdated books from large universities and libraries (which would otherwise go to a landfill), repackages them, and sells them online globally, sharing the proceeds with the universities and libraries. The ReStore on Gasoline Alley in Springfield, Massachusetts (one of Joe's incubations), accepts surplus and outdated building materials from large manufacturers and materials from home remodeling projects, deconstructs homes and repackages the materials, sells the products to economically challenged neighborhoods, and builds homes for the homeless with Habitat for Humanity and with Hampden County House of Corrections inmates. These are all partnerships that were generated through the ideals of sustainability.

CREATE PEACE OF MIND

When you are doing the right thing for the environment and humanity, your mind is not plagued by guilt or fear of being caught operating in a way that is in conflict with the common good. You sleep better.

Now that we've reviewed the many advantages of sustainability, let's get started making your business more sustainable.

1

Leadership—
Greening from the Top

No single factor is more important to successfully greening an enterprise than for its leaders to create a sustainability vision and make a commitment to continuous progress toward realizing that vision. This chapter is about finding that vision, owning it, articulating it, and getting your managers and employees to support it so that your sustainability goals become their sustainability goals. Once this is done, the vision is infused into the corporate culture and becomes self-replicating.

In creating Stonyfield Farm, CEO Gary Hirshberg had a vision that "the company is not about making yogurt but about greening the world one yogurt container at a time."[1] Horst Rechelbacher of Aveda had a vision of using 100 percent organic ingredients, not petrochemicals, in nonfood products such as cosmetics because doing so is better for the health of the planet and your health too.

Today, both of these companies have hundreds of millions of dollars in annual sales and are mostly owned by multinational conglomerates, but they both started out as struggling little companies. Their mission of healing the planet led to their success. Now they are transforming the multibillion dollar multinational companies that invested in them into more sustainable companies.

Creating a Vision

The first step in leading a company into the pursuit of sustainability is to create a vision that says "this is who we are, this is what we stand for, so this is what we do." If you are an entrepreneur, this vision is generally born in your head. The exercise of developing the vision becomes a fun opportunity to communicate your hopes, dreams, and aspirations and define the role you want to play in healing the planet while serving employees, customers, investors, and other stakeholders. Some companies develop their vision using a collaborative brainstorming process with the employees. Some companies even bring in facilitators to ensure that the process taps into all the company's brainpower, pulling input from soft-spoken team members as well as the ones who always make themselves heard. Although it might seem that visions collaboratively created would have better buy-in from employees, those crafted solely by the entrepreneurial visionary can work equally well.

Once you have the vision, capture it in writing by creating a simple mission statement, which can consist of merely a few lines. The mission statement should not list specific numerical goals, technologies, or tactics to accomplish the mission. Details like these become self-limiting and don't anticipate how far and fast boundaries can be pushed when an organization rallies around its mission.

Once the mission statement is prepared, post it prominently on your Web site, on company letterhead, on invoices and purchase orders, on the back of your business card, and on a sign at the front door greeting employees and visitors. The more public the vision is, the harder it will be for you not to live up to it.

For many, the vision begins when they encounter a problem and begin to seek a solution. Gary's vision began to form before he started Stonyfield, while he was executive director of the New Alchemy Institute, a sustainability technology think tank.

Horst was a world-famous hair stylist who had built his business from the ground up. He explains, "I was the chemist, the salesman, the packaging designer, and the designer and spokesperson of the mission." He and his hair stylist colleagues were getting sick from the toxic chemicals they were using on their clients' hair. Horst's mother, an apothecary, visited him from their native Austria and said, "Don't you smell how bad your salon smells from all these chemicals?" From then on Horst committed himself to work at healing his impact on the planet. He recalls, "I said to myself, 'I can fix that. I can make this a little bit different.' Then I went to India to get another point of view and studied Yoga and Ayurvedic medicine, particularly inhalation therapy, and I came back with a clear vision for Aveda." That vision was repeated over and over and became the foundation on which Aveda was built.[2]

ABC Home is the premier furniture and home furnishings company in New York. After her daughter started school, its founder, Paulette Mae Cole, came back to run it with the intention of making ABC Home more sustainable. As Paulette describes the work of greening her company, "I talk vision all the time. Communication is important because it is the only way you can mentor and model and articulate your mission. We try to express to people that 'home' is our mirror. Home is how we reflect our vision and values to the planet. Our collective home, the planet, is a mirror reflection of humanity. It mirrors us and speaks directly to us who we are. We speak to and seek new consumers who vote with their dollars and have their values reflected in their homes. To me, every aspect of what we are doing in moving toward sustainability is very powerful. In the baby and bed departments we have organic beds as an alternative to people having their heads on a bed for eight hours every day that is outgassing toxic chemicals. We stopped selling paraffin candles. We installed air purifiers throughout the stores and then started selling them. We reuse all the packaging material, and that is especially difficult since most of our items are one of a kind. The wood in our furniture is now sustainably harvested. It is incredibly impactful. It's a huge cultural shift that was very challenging, and our only hope of getting this to work with all the people working for us is to constantly articulate the vision." Paulette started ABC Home with a vision and ideals and has created a $100 million enterprise.[3]

Taking Responsibility

Many entrepreneurial companies are one-person operations where the owner, as "chief cook and bottle washer," also handles the sustainability issues. As an organization expands, responsibilities are divided. But many socially responsible entrepreneurs remain the keeper of the responsibilities associated with being green even as their organizations grow to a point where they have many direct reports. Doug Hammond, president of Relief Resources, which had over 3,000 employees, was chiefly responsible for his company's sustainability practices mostly because he found it the most challenging and exciting task in his organization.

But if your business gets large enough that you do assign someone else to be the keeper of sustainable practices, you still need to take ultimate responsibility for ensuring that the vision is realized. This means that the person needs to report directly to the most senior management and the board of directors and must be allowed to always speak the truth. What the senior management and the board do with that information is for them to decide, but the organization's leaders need to know what is going on.

When Horst appointed Aveda's first director of ecological affairs and sustainability, Terry Gips, who previously had worked with the Carter administration, he instructed Terry to report to the planet, not the CEO.

Having a well-organized reporting structure is critical. For example, to eliminate plastic packaging for the furniture items ABC Home sold and delivered, the company decided to invest in a huge number of reusable packing blankets. It did not have a reporting structure in place, however, and at the end of six months, all the blankets were gone.

Living Your Vision

Once you articulate the vision and take responsibility for it, you need to live that vision. If you drive a Hummer, don't turn out the lights in your office when you leave, and don't recycle your paper, your team will ignore you. "Do as I say, not as I do" does not work. That's the old model of authoritative hierarchy.

To be successful, you have to model the vision at least in some form. Horst uses his products, comments on your "chemical" smell if you don't use them, and drives a Tesla electric car. Windmills power his company. Renewable energy company Real Goods' founder, John Schaeffer, built and lives in a home completely powered by renewable energy. Jirka Rysavy, founder of Gaiam, lives in a home without electricity and running water. Gary Hirshberg built his home from trees he sustainably harvested on his land. Sustainability economist Hazel Henderson wears only preworn clothes bought in thrift shops. Joe rides his bike back and forth to Gasoline Alley,

CSRwire.com, and local meetings (thirteen miles each way). All of these successful leaders walk their talk in one way or another, and these apparent idiosyncrasies are their currency for authenticity. It's great for employees to see some behavior in their principal that stands out and communicates in no uncertain terms "I really mean what I say about sustainability."

Living the vision also means being true to your beliefs in your business. Greg Steltenpohl, founder and former CEO of Odwalla, noted, "The employees see what you have to go through to realize your vision, and they see how much extra work it takes to do the right thing. When they see that you don't take the easy way out and you live your vision, it changes them."[4]

Greg's vision included a need to find a solution to the plastic bottles used for his product. Santa Cruz was the largest market for Odwalla products in the company's infancy. The city did not have a plastic recycling program, and Greg did not want to see his plastic bottle in the landfills in this community. Greg recalls, "I went to the city and county and suggested they put in place a plastic recycling program and offered to find a market for the plastic. Then I said to the officials, 'If we collect our own bottles and set up a recycling system, buy the equipment to crush the plastic, and find a market for the plastic, will you be our partner?' And they said yes. After that the entire city of Santa Cruz started recycling. We attracted a lot of press and a lot of customers from this, and sales increased incredibly."[5]

Making Your Vision Stick

Your organization will begin to transform once you come up with a vision, articulate that commitment, live it, and create a sustainability reporting structure. It's almost like having a magic wand, but not quite. There's still hard work to do, too. Gary recalls,

> I often joke that we are a twenty-six-year overnight success. Greening a company is a work in progress. There were a lot of doubters in the early days. They thought that I was this liberal, crazy person. These doubters were foot draggers. They drove my sister Nancy, who was in charge of sustainability from the get-go, crazy. There was all this passive-aggressive behavior.
>
> I am happy to say that I don't have any of these people now. They did not leave; they came around. In most cases we were right on all the things we wanted to do, like sourcing milk exclusively from local family farms with rBGH [recombinant bovine growth hormone] free cows. We were right about going organic, even though at the time it cost 100 percent more to source organic ingredients. The employees have seen other brands that did not follow us fail. Or they saw how much more other companies had to spend on advertising. We built not just loyal customers but maniacally loyal customers. The employees saw how energy costs and health insurance costs climbed as we predicted.
>
> The folks that were the hardest to convert were the engineers. They were taught that 'the solution to pollution is dilution' and they thought what we were trying to accomplish was a dope-smoke rant. Then we built a wastewater treatment plant that produced methane and less sludge, and we made money. They saw that what we were doing was not just about the environment but also about job security. We won the battle of converting the employees over time by evidence, not by rhetoric.

We were basically challenging everything they knew, so it took a long time for their preconceived beliefs to die and for them to accept doing things in a different way. This is all now in the DNA here.[6]

At Aveda, Horst did not run a top-down, command-and-control organization. The company used group management with majority rule. Horst said, "I always encouraged the teams to outvote me and to fight for what they believed in. I said, 'Let me tell you what I want and you convince me that it is not good,' and then we have majority rule and that was fine for me. Inspiration was important to me. I would work to inspire the people and then experience that which I inspired. I would encourage everyone to look at our products holistically—learn how the product is made and how the ingredients are grown."[7]

Brent Baker of TriState Biodiesel has a similar story about inspiration:

I was an environmental activist. In 1995 I was traveling as part of a national tour I created to promote the challenges of global warming. On the tour was a bunch of women who called themselves the VegeBabes with a tour bus powered by biodiesel. They had a bunch of magnetic signs with the logos of McDonald's, Burger King, Wendy's, Taco Bell, and Kentucky Fried Chicken that they slapped on the side of their bus, and they stopped at those fast-food places along the tour, telling the franchisees and managers that they were sanctioned by headquarters to pick up the used fry oil to power the bus as a way of promoting the parent company. Then they cooked the biodiesel in the back of the bus using Bunsen burners, methanol, and Drano. They never bought gas and the bus made a sweet-smelling exhaust that was lower in pollution than diesel, and that's when I decided to get into the biodiesel business.

I love having people come to work here who don't know anything about environmentalism. They listen to my presentations to prospective clients and get inspired when they learn what we're about. Then I love to hear them give the story to others, and I get inspired.[8]

Motivating Employees to Buy In

Inspiring employees to buy in to the sustainability vision is key to becoming sustainable. Invite all of them to be on the winning team and to help the team cross the finish line to victory and they will do everything within their power and ability to conspire for success.

At Odwalla this inspiration extended beyond the company. Greg recalls, "We hired, trained, and motivated people to be managers who at first did not know anything about sustainability. At the time, we did not realize that we were creating managers who would become leaders in their own sustainable organizations. Twenty years later, the leaders we created went on to inspire other leaders. If we were to calculate the impact all these leaders had, their combined impacts would dwarf our impact."[9]

It's imperative to get your entire team aligned with the standards the organization adopts and against which it will be measured. This is not difficult to do. We have found, at least in dealing with implementation and management of sustainability systems, that employees' motivation follows the rules for Maslow's Motivational Hierarchy.

Abraham Maslow submitted that there is a motivational hierarchy starting with people's requirement that their basic needs (e.g., food, shelter) be met. Only when their basic needs are met can they then be motivated upward to the next level of the motivational hierarchy, safety, which includes security of body, employment, family, and health.[10]

The next factor is belonging, the joy we get from friends, family, and peers. Then comes esteem, the sense of personal accomplishment and the witnessing of one's accomplishments by others within and outside an organization.

The final motivational factor is self-actualization. At this level, people combine their personal goals with those of their organization, develop creativity, and become proactive problem solvers.

If people's needs are interrupted anywhere along the motivational hierarchy, they are demotivated down to the next lower level. So, for example, even if a company does a great job of encouraging belonging and esteem, if it has policies that are seen as unfair (safety), the employees will never be motivated beyond the level of meeting their basic needs.

A company takes care of basic needs with salary. Security needs are addressed with fair and just company policies, health insurance, pensions, management training, and, among other things, the pursuit of sustainability. It communicates that the company actually does care about employees, their families, the community, customers, and the entire stakeholder community, including the planet. This helps motivate employees up the hierarchy.

The motivational hierarchy has nothing to do with the organizational hierarchy, whether an organization has democratic or autocratic governance. And whether democratic or autocratic, management must try to motivate employees to function at their highest level of motivation. Not everyone responds to motivational techniques, however. About 10 percent of people are already self-actualizers and don't need to be motivated. Another 10 percent do not respond to any sort of motivation. The middle 80 percent can be motivated up or down depending on what management does.

One way to motivate employees is to reward them with company-wide recognition for pointing out areas for sustainability improvement. Mention them in a company-wide e-mail. Put their names and pictures up on a bulletin board. Give them a trophy or some other prize, or offer them the most coveted parking spot with the sign "Our Sustainability Hero of the Month."

Every organization has lots of "low-hanging fruit"—opportunities for sustainability improvement that are very cost-effective and easy to implement. And highlighting the employees who find these opportunities addresses their and their peers' needs for safety, belonging, and esteem. When they become "local heroes," employees get addicted to picking fruit. Once they pick all the low-hanging fruit, they become incredibly creative and innovative in identifying and picking the higher, more-difficult-to-reach fruit.

Another way to incentivize employees is through the creation of mutually agreed-upon measures of performance (MOPs). This works because when performance measures are collaboratively arrived at and objective, instead of subjective, employees feel safe.

At Stonyfield, environmental performance criteria are very much a part of pay, bonuses, and promotion. Aveda used bonuses and overseas trips as incentives for meeting environmental goals.

In chapter 3, we talk about how you can convert your vision into a plan, but to do that, you need to know where you currently are. Now that your vision has been articulated and embraced by your team, it's time to determine where you really are on the road to sustainability. In the next chapter, we will discuss sustainability audits and how to do them. By measuring where you are, you will know what you need to do to implement your vision.

Summary

Leaders must have a clear vision of where they want to go, be able to articulate the vision, attach the necessary controls and measures, inspire through their own actions, and accept that continuous improvement leads to success. A clear statement like "greening the world one yogurt container at a time" or "report the results of our actions to the planet" helps your team understand the vision in one phrase or sentence.

The most powerful actions you can take as an entrepreneur to lead your organization along the path of sustainability are these:

- Draft and then articulate your sustainability vision.
- Take responsibility for realizing the vision. If you have a person who is assigned the task of managing sustainability, make sure that person reports directly to you (the boss) and the board of directors.
- Personally live that vision in and out of the office.
- Make your sustainability vision stick through inspiration and by providing evidence of its effectiveness.
- Motivate your employees to support the sustainability mission.

Audits—
Measuring Where You Are

Whatever sustainability target you have set for yourself, in order to hit the bull's-eye you have to know where you are standing in relation to your target. The process for assessing your current sustainability performance is called a *sustainability audit*. In a sustainability audit, you try to quantify your energy and material use and your emissions and releases to the environment. You also seek objective evidence to assess whether you are in compliance with regulations and any voluntary commitments that you have made vis-à-vis the environment or sustainability. A sustainability audit is your environmental report card.

Every line item in your profit (and loss) statement, cash flow statement, general ledger, and balance sheet has a corresponding environmental impact. The sustainability audit quantifies that impact. While a sustainability audit is a look backward, it is a crucial step in moving forward toward sustainability. To get where you are going, you have to know where you are. Creating a plan helps you find what additional key measures you need to assess. After the audit, you may discover items that should be included in your plan.

This chapter explains the elements of a successful general sustainability audit and provides information on how to carry out an audit and create an audit report to convey the results and meaning of the audit. The audit report communicates to your organization its state of sustainability so that you can manage your course in making continuous improvement toward environmental excellence.

Subsequent chapters deal with details of more expansive sustainability audits, including the input/output mass balance analysis (IOMBA), life cycle analysis, break-even analysis (chapter 4), energy audit (chapter 7), and carbon emissions audit (chapter 8). Collectively, these audits measure your organization's environmental performance so that you can make the necessary improvements to become more sustainable.

The first measure to take is our favorite and the most important part of any sustainability audit—the confidential employee questionnaire. It surveys employees' perceptions of the company's environmental practices. We recommend sending the questionnaire to every full- and part-time employee. Make sure the questionnaire is translated into as many languages as your employees speak. The key to getting valid responses is to provide for complete confidentiality. You can place this questionnaire online using one of the many (sometimes free) survey tools, such as SurveyMonkey[1] or Zoomerang.[2] However, to make sure that those employees who do not use computers can also fill out the questionnaire, provide a printed version in a preaddressed, stamped envelope (or have a locked suggestion box in the office where they can leave the survey without being noticed). Leave adequate space for employees to write their answers on the survey.

A sample survey questionnaire is provided in resource A. Your business may be specialized enough so that it needs additional questions in order to get a valid assessment of your company's sustainability profile, but we don't recommend adding more than three questions to the survey.

The questionnaire should be accompanied by a cover letter placed on company letterhead and signed by the organization's top leader so that the importance of filling out the questionnaire honestly and completely is very clear.

In most cases, this employee questionnaire will provide some of the most valuable information (good and bad) you will get out of the whole audit process. For example, 80 percent of the employees at one fossil-fuel power plant agreed with the statement, "Management would knowingly violate environmental and human rights laws." That is important information for a company's senior management to know. In this case it was a wake-up call, and the managers subsequently did the work necessary to clean up their act and win back their employees' confidence. For most companies we've engaged in this process, the employees' recommendations have been right on target.

Evaluating Survey Responses

For yes/no or multiple-choice questions, determine what percentage of employees responded the same way. When scoring the open-ended employee questions, assign a word or two to summarize each response and sort the responses into "strengths," "weaknesses," and "recommendations." For example, if one person says, "The company uses energy conservatively"; another writes, "Electrical usage per unit of output is managed well"; and a third says, "Our plant is energy efficient," they're all saying the same thing, so score this as three votes for "energy efficient" as a strength. "Wastes energy" may summarize several responses that count as weaknesses, and "install energy-efficient lighting" may summarize several recommendations. Then when scoring, see how many "energy efficient" responses you have under strengths, "wastes energy" under weaknesses, and "install energy-efficient lighting" under recommendations.

What you should do with that information is like the punch line of the joke "If one person calls you a horse, laugh it off; if two people call you a horse, think about it; and if three people call you a horse, shop for a saddle." You might get a lot of individual wacky comments, but if three or more people point out the same weakness or recommendation, you probably have a real problem or a least a real communication problem you need to address.

The fundamental tenet of all sustainability work is that your most valuable corporate assets are your employees. An employee who has been with a company for ten years and at the same workstation for five, for example, may know a lot more about the company's impact on the planet than a professional auditor who spends only minutes assessing that same workstation. For this reason, someone should interview (face-to-face) a statistical sampling of all employees and every employee who is a key part of implementing the company's sustainability plan. These confidential interviews should include 100 percent of senior management.

Vendors and their employees should be included in the survey to get a complete picture of your company's total environmental performance. The vendor survey is covered in chapter 9.

It is best to issue the survey questionnaire first and then use the results to create your audit protocol. The survey results will help you identify the areas you should be investigating when you perform the audit. For example, if ten employees tell you that the maintenance foreperson is dumping used oil down the drain, that is something you should investigate in your audit.

Creating the Audit Protocol

The next step in performing a general sustainability audit is to create an audit protocol—a list of the items that you are going to audit. An audit protocol usually begins with evaluating whether a company is in compliance with regulations and all of the environmental goals it has set for itself. An audit will generally also measure all the parameters that are environmentally impactful, such as emissions to air, releases to water, and solid waste (with quantification of the amount of material reused and recycled). Resource B contains a sample audit protocol.

In order to make continuous improvement in becoming sustainable, you have to create a baseline and measure where you are at a certain time and place. So the first sustainability audit is called a baseline audit. Once the baseline has been established and your boundaries have been clearly defined, you can use them as the basis for making improvements.

How do you know the effectiveness of your conservation efforts? By measuring how much, for example, energy and water you used last year and how much you are using after you implement your conservation efforts. If you state that the company is working to reduce greenhouse gas emissions, your audit results will quantify your emissions and verify that fact. If you have a policy that says that 10 percent of profits go to the planet, then your audit results will determine if you are keeping this commitment.

In an audit you can take direct measurements (like testing the indoor air for formaldehyde; measuring releases to water of phosphorus; measuring smokestack gas emissions of nitrogen oxide [NO_x]; and measuring gallons of water, oil, or kilowatt-hours used). You can also do quantification through indirect measurements, extrapolation, and estimation. For example, many facilities assess their wastewater quantity by measuring not their wastewater flow but the amount of fresh water they consume because if potable water enters the building, the same quantity, plus or minus a bit, has to leave the building as wastewater. Similarly, a reliable estimate of carbon dioxide emissions can be made by multiplying the number of gallons of gasoline used by the 19 pounds of carbon dioxide produced per gallon of gasoline combusted or even by using fleet miles-per-gallon figures to estimate CO_2 emissions based on miles traveled.

You can also measure for surrogates. For example, milk is hard to measure when it is mixed with other ingredients as it is made mostly of water with protein, sugar, and fat. But whole milk is 3.5 percent fat, so you can measure the milk fat and then multiply by 100/3.5 to find out how much milk is used or lost at various process points. In this case, milk fat is a surrogate measure for milk. In the same way, you can count the number of cups used at a fast-food restaurant to get a very accurate idea of not only how much soda was drunk but even how many hamburgers were eaten in that same time period.

Another audit methodology is to research the paper trail to determine levels of performance and compliance. For example, instead of directly metering your electricity, you can look at your electric bills. Organic food, as another example, is not certified by testing the food for traces of synthetic fertilizer, pesticides, and herbicides. Certification is done by auditing the paper trail of the farm. Similarly, you can do a paper/electronic inventory of your raw materials instead of doing a physical inventory.

Keys to an Effective Audit

You will have a very effective sustainability audit if you follow these steps:

1. Survey the employees and report on the findings of that survey in terms of what they saw as the company's strengths and weaknesses, how they rated management in terms of encouraging environmentally responsible behavior, and what recommendations they offered.
2. Use the employee survey to pinpoint which areas you should investigate and validate in the audit.
3. Quantify energy use, water use, and material use as well as emissions to air, releases to water, and solid waste. The solids should be broken out into how much material is diverted from landfills (i.e., recycled, reused, composted).
4. Qualify that the company is in compliance with all relevant environmental regulations and its own commitments in sustainability. This means finding objective evidence to affirm or deny every statement the company makes relating to the environment. If the company says its products are all natural, validate that. If it says that 10 percent of profits go to support environmental activities, confirm whether that is the case. For example, if the company says that its products are "environmentally friendly," determine if that is true. (Hint: "environmentally friendly" is a subjective term that cannot be validated. Its use violates the terms of the Federal Trade Commission and EPA's "Guides for the Use of Environmental Marketing Claims"[3] and violates truth-in-advertising laws.)

The only thing that would make the audit significantly more effective is if it measured the gap between where the company currently is and where it would be if the company had zero impact directly as well as indirectly (through its vendors).

Heisenberg's indeterminacy principle, one of the laws of physics, states that you can't measure anything without changing it. And this is true for an audit. However, it is also true that performing an audit motivates employees. This is probably due to what is called the Hawthorne Effect, named after a study of the employees at Western Electric's Hawthorne plant in Illinois. The company tried to determine the relationship between lighting levels and productivity. In the study, when the lighting was increased, productivity went up. When it was increased again, productivity went up again. When the study was completed and the lighting was set back to the original levels, productivity went up again. The study showed that the biggest impact on productivity was not the lighting level but the survey itself, which effectively articulated to the workers that management was interested in what motivated them.[4]

Horst Rechelbacher of Aveda discusses how the sustainability audit got the whole company involved. "It was like an outside-inside reunion. It really made the employees and the members of the different teams feel connected. The audit findings became a reward in and of themselves. That is why the money for the audit was so well spent. The audit was like a vitamin shot in the arm. It really uplifted the company. We discussed it at our yearly events and the congresses of the various Aveda salons around the world. We introduced the audit findings to our employees, salon owners, and affiliates. It was the best thing for business. Third-party auditing, where you have outsiders take a look inside, needs to be part of the mantra for every business."[5]

With this said, an audit also disrupts the day-to-day routine. It takes a significant amount of management and employee time that would otherwise be dedicated to producing revenue. So don't do an audit every year. Some companies do one every two years and some audit just critical functions every year and facilities every five years.

To minimize disruption, combine other audits with your sustainability audit. For example, companies that get audited to the ISO 9000 total quality management standard may also get their ISO 14000 Environmental Management Systems audit done at the same time. ISO 9000 and 14000 are covered in chapter 3. If you are going to audit other parameters often covered under a broader definition of sustainability or social responsibility, do it while you are conducting your environmental audit. This can include auditing for diversity, living wage, work-life balance, employee empowerment, spirituality in business, governance, talk-do gap (the disparity between what you say and what you do), fair trade/organics, workers' rights, charitable giving, and corporate-sponsored social/environmental activism.

Third-Party Audits

When an audit is performed internally, it is called an internal audit. When independent outsiders come in to perform the audit, it is called a third-party audit. Anyone within your organization (even you) who performs the audit has a stake in the outcome. When you have a stake in the results, it is hard to be objective, and objectivity is key to the success of any audit. Therefore, someone who will neither get fired nor get promoted as a result of the audit findings should ideally do the audit.

Consider having the audit performed by an objective third party who has experience in auditing environmental and social parameters. If you don't want to bring in a third party to conduct the entire audit, consider hiring someone to process the confidential employee questionnaires and to conduct follow-up interviews of a statistically significant number (5–10 percent) of employees and all key managers to validate the findings in the questionnaires. A third-party audit will cost anywhere between $5,000 and $50,000 per facility depending on your organization's size, the nature of your business (e.g. service company versus chemical manufacturer), the complexity of the audit, and who (and how many whos) is doing it.

Laury Hammel, owner of the Longfellow Clubs, pioneered a novel type of third-party audit for the Social Venture Network that avoided hiring a third-party auditor. Laury was the founder of the New England Business Association for Social Responsibility, which later became Business for Social Responsibility (BSR). He put together five pairs of noncompeting business owners with similar-sized companies. Auditing against the SVN Standards of Corporate Social Responsibility, an audit team from one company audited the other and vice versa. The only costs were for travel expenses and assignment of staff time.

Preparing the Audit Report

When preparing the report, make a one- to two-page executive summary of the key findings, including a table of the key metrics and recommendations. The rest of the report should cover the following topics (depending on their relevance to your particular company/organization):

- Energy use, carbon footprint, and conservation
- Water use and conservation
- Material use and conservation
- Manufacturing, service procedures, and retail operations
- Packaging
- Transportation, distribution, and commuting
- Emissions to air, releases to water, and pollution prevention—recycling, reuse, and disposal
- Physical plant issues
- Procurement practices and requirements of subcontractors and vendors
- Design for the environment and sustainability

- Regulatory compliance
- Corporate communications
- Environmental and sustainability management systems
- Environmental risk and hazard preparedness
- Employee issues
- Global/ecological impacts

For each of these categories, the audit report should be structured to detail strengths, weaknesses, opportunities, threats, and recommendations (SWOTR).

Every company we've worked with that has had a sustainability audit has invariably made money in the process. Almost always, after we report the results and the company implements the recommendations, the leaders quietly tell us how much money they are making from reduced costs of goods, reduced energy costs, reduced absenteeism, increased productivity, or increased sales and market share.

What to Do with Your Audit Results

It is hard to recommend actions to take until you complete the sustainability audit, but some general recommendations include the following:

- Make some kind of graphical representations of your energy, water, and material use for the baseline year and for each successive year and show these parameters as a function of the number of units shipped or sales dollars (adjusted for inflation). Include as much granularity in each category as you can so that, for example, energy is not a lump sum but divided into manageable subcategories such as energy use for manufacturing operations, transportation/distribution, commuting, and facility maintenance.

- Distribute the report's executive summary so that employees and other stakeholders can read it. Act on at least a few of the weaknesses and a few of the recommendations reported by large numbers of employees.
- As soon as you practically can, remedy the areas where you are in noncompliance with regulations or your own stated commitments. Note: to encourage environmental audits, forty-three states and the federal government provide amnesty and prosecutorial immunity for regulatory noncompliance issues that are discovered in a voluntary audit process, providing that the noncompliances were not the result of an intent to violate the law and that they are cured in a "timely manner." This generally means becoming compliant at a rate that does not put the company at a financial risk.[6]
- Pick targets for where you will be making measurable continuous improvement and cost savings.

Summary

The sustainability audit is your environmental report card and establishes where you are in relation to your current energy and material use, emissions and releases to the environment, regulatory and voluntary commitments, and your overall environmental impact. The audit can be completed in-house or through a third party. Either way, your employees are critical contributors to the audit; give them plenty of room to express themselves and inspire their support of the process. Preparing an audit protocol that identifies all the areas you wish to audit, interviewing vendors and their employees, selecting a third-party auditor, and auditing against predetermined standards (like the ISO 9000 and ISO 14000) and against other standards (like the SVN standards or standards that you create) are key decisions to make. Analyze your results and accept these results as the baseline for improvements.

These are the key steps to a successful sustainability audit:

- Perform a confidential survey of your employees to assess their perception of the company's sustainability strengths and weaknesses.
- Use the results of this survey to create an audit protocol.
- Perform the audit to quantify and qualify environmental performance.
- Prepare an audit report with an executive summary of strengths, weaknesses, opportunities, threats, and recommendations.
- Implement recommendations, especially the ones that are cost-effective and that make your company compliant with its vision.

In the next chapter we explore how you convert your vision into a plan. Existing standards, protocols, and frameworks are discussed and instructions for creating the plan are conveyed.

The Plan—
Implementing Your
Sustainability Vision

You have your vision, it's authentic, and it resonates with your actions. You have buy-in from the employees and a mechanism to motivate them to work toward continuous environmental improvement. You have performed a baseline audit and are informed of all the key events that influence your company's environmental footprint. Now you need a plan to translate that vision into action. Once you have a *plan*, you can *do* what the plan requires of you, *measure* the results of your action, and then *review* the results to determine if you are on target or need to tweak the plan in order to keep making continuous progress toward sustainability.

This chapter is about converting your sustainability vision into a plan and ensuring its success by *planning, doing, measuring, and reviewing.* You'll learn how to determine which of the various environmental management systems, protocols, and standards can best help you achieve your vision. Whatever options you select and whatever direction you take, don't seek perfection because it is perennially elusive. Seek excellence and push yourself and your organization, but aim for continuous improvement, not perfection.

In order to convert their mission to action, the leaders of Stonyfield Farm created teams of employees. "At Stonyfield the employees take their mission so seriously now," Gary Hirshberg said. "We have created a Mission Action Program (MAP), which is how we make sure our mission comes to life. The MAP teams are made up of diverse members from every sector of the company. We have ten teams with each focusing on different aspects of sustainability. We have a water team that is concentrating on reducing our water use. The water team has engineers on it but also marketing people. A packaging team is working to reduce the weight of packaging material.

"The ten teams report to the executive team monthly. In addition, there are twice-annual summits where all the teams report their achievements and challenges. These probably influence internal culture as much as anything else we do. Nancy and I can talk all we want, but the people in operations have more impact on our environmental footprint, and they're the ones on the MAP teams. They are hacking away at reducing all of our metrics: energy use, carbon footprint, water use, packaging material use, on-farm impact, etc. We also have Problem Solving Groups (PSGs). Pretty much everybody in the company has environmental criteria as part of their job responsibilities."[1]

Gary is a big believer in "if you can measure it, you can manage it," and each one of these MAP teams makes a plan, executes the plan, measures the results, and then reviews the success of its actions.

"Plan, Do, Measure, and Review" was not born at Stonyfield. It actually comes from a movement toward quality management invented by American women working in wartime factories during World War II.

Total Quality Management

Prior to WWII, the quality of America's military equipment and munitions production was poor. Duds were common.

After Pearl Harbor, when men left the factories to go fight, women arrived to run the factories. The women had a big stake in the quality of work. If they made a mistake, their brothers, fathers, husbands, and friends would suffer on the battlefield.

To improve quality, the women closely inspected each item, not just at the end of the assembly line but at the beginning as well. Instead of competing, they had the manufacturing lines cooperate with one another. At the end of the workday, on their own time, they sat in circles to discuss quality. From their hearts and out of necessity, they created the Quality Circle.

In this new management environment, productivity improved dramatically. Improvement was so significant that statisticians were sent into the factories to investigate. A statistician named W. Edwards Deming "discovered" the Quality Circle system that the women had created. In his report, he recommended that the women and their system remain after the men came home from the war.

After the war, business boomed. Like many members of society with unorthodox ideas challenging conventional wisdom, Deming was strongly urged to "get out of town." He left the United States and landed in Japan. After a period of investigation and review, he integrated the Zen Buddhist sensibilities of the Japanese culture with what he had learned from the American women and adjusted his philosophy. The Buddhist idea of community—Sarigha[2]—was introduced into the workplace along with Deming's Buddhist-inspired dictum "Eliminate fear from the workplace."

In Japan, the Quality Circle methodology evolved. The Japanese had a word for this body of work: Kaizen—"continuous improvement." This nation that made products that were laughed at evolved a management methodology that put the American automotive business into receivership years later.

This method, generically called Total Quality Management (TQM), was then exported to the United States and elsewhere.

The precepts of TQM were codified into a global standard for the International Standards Organization (ISO) called ISO 9000. If they elect to, companies can prepare their organizations to meet the criteria of ISO 9000. Then they are audited against the standard's criteria. If they meet all the criteria, they become ISO 9000 certified for a period of time by a certifying organization. The basic concept behind ISO 9000 is that business owners and employees need to act as if the customer is king or queen. In order to satisfy the customer, a business has to make continuous improvements. The pathway to making continuous improvements is to Plan, Do, Measure, and Review while involving the entire stakeholder community. Chief among this stakeholder community are the employees. They are viewed not as cogs in the machine or expendable soldiers on the battlefield but as human beings who are the key to a company realizing its vision.

In the 1970s when the Japanese auto industry began to dominate U.S. automakers, Ford was the first company to commit to making an ISO 9000 Total Quality Management automobile, adopting the motto "Quality Is Job One" and designing the Taurus, which won all kinds of design awards and lots of business for Ford. Not to be outdone, both GM and Chrysler created ISO 9000 cars.

Focused on quality, ISO 9000 nonetheless allowed these companies to cost-effectively introduce a myriad of environmental quality innovations, such as greater fuel efficiency, volatile organic compound (VOC) free paints, and reduction or even elimination of the use of hazardous chemicals. All of these innovations were made possible by rigorous adherence to the ISO 9000 principles of Plan, Do, Measure, and Review. ISO 9000 works for big companies, but it also works for small and medium-sized companies. It has tremendous value to companies even if they do not get certified but merely use the standard as a guide. One aspect of TQM is total environmental quality management or sustainability management.

ISO 14000

In the 1990s ISO 9000 gave birth to a total *environmental* quality management standard, ISO 14000. David is an ISO 9000 lead auditor who was one of a handful of Americans who represented the United States and ANSI at the UN at the outset in the creation of ISO 14000. Today it is the most widely implemented set of standards for environmental management systems (EMSs). An increasing number of companies, including small and medium-sized companies, are embracing ISO 14000 worldwide. ISO 14000, like ISO 9000, is actually a suite of standards. Whether you elect to get certified or not, giving management attention to the component parts of ISO 14000 will greatly advance you toward sustainability.

One straightforward way to convert your vision into a sustainability plan is to follow the steps to compliance with ISO 14000. This does not necessarily mean getting certified, but it does mean investing management and employee time in addressing the requirements. What ISO 14000 asks of you is to first *create an environmental policy* (from your vision). This can be as simple as "We commit ourselves to reducing the amount of water we use and greenhouse gases we produce." The next step is to *determine the environmental aspects and impacts of all of your products, activities, and services* (more on how to do this in chapter 4). Then you *plan environmental objectives and measurable targets*. This is where you commit, for example, to reducing water use by 30 percent per year (250,000 gallons per day) while still being able to grow output by 10 percent per year. The next step is to *implement and operate programs to meet the objectives and targets*; then you *check compliance, take corrective action, and conduct management review.* Resource C covers the seventeen specific elements that make up ISO 14001. If you want even more detail you can buy and download a copy of the standard from ISO.[3]

Do-it-yourself ISO 14000 software is available for $700 to $2,700.[4] The costs of ISO 14000 implementation and certification can vary greatly depending on the size of a facility and the nature of its operation. For small to medium-sized manufacturing facilities (i.e., 100–300 employees) the cost of developing and auditing an EMS will generally range from $20,000 to $50,000.[5] ISO 14000 is really transforming the landscape and pushing more and more companies and organizations globally to pursue sustainability profitably.[6] But even if you just create a formal procedure in your organization for addressing each of the above steps, you will have advanced your company far in pursuing sustainability. This is because ISO 14000 makes you do the hard work of figuring out the environmental aspects and impacts of your products, activities, and services.

If, however, your company does not manufacture products with a potentially severe environmental impact and you are looking for perhaps an easier course than ISO 14000, consider the CERES Principles.

CERES Principles

The CERES Principles had their origin in the Valdez Principles, which were created in the wake of the *Exxon Valdez* oil spill disaster in Prince William Sound off Valdez, Alaska. The Valdez Principles were designed to provide a framework of corporate environmental management to ensure that environmental disasters are prevented and that companies are proactive instead of reactive in regard to the environment. The Valdez Principles—cocreated by Denis Hayes of Earth Day fame and the late Joan Bavaria, founder of Trillium Asset Management and an innovator in socially responsible investing—became the CERES Principles.[7] CERES's current chair is Norman Dean, previously executive director of Green Seal and Friends of the Earth, and its executive director is Mindy Lubber.[8] If you like these principles, make them yours. You can even join CERES and formalize your relationship with these principles. (CERES has a sliding membership cost starting at $2,000.)

The CERES Principles cover protection of the biosphere, sustainable use of natural resources, reduction and disposal of wastes, energy conservation, risk reduction, safe products and services, environmental restoration, and informing the public. CERES requires the same level of leadership commitment as is recommended in chapter 1 and, as is recommended in chapter 2, requires audits and reports. CERES, however, mandates that these reports be made available to the public.

CERES has just published its *21st Century Corporation: The CERES Roadmap for Sustainability* "as a vision and practical roadmap for integrating sustainability into the DNA of business—from the boardroom to the copy room."[9] The twenty key expectations for companies cover governance for sustainability, stakeholder engagement, disclosure, and performance.

"Mine was the first company to sign onto CERES," recalls Horst Rechelbacher of Aveda. "I came to the first meeting of the Valdez Principles and I was sitting with my friends Paul Hawken and Terry Gips and a bunch of investment bankers, corporate lawyers, investment groups, and other business owners, and the consensus was that we need to govern ourselves by the Valdez Principles. The principles were all written out and I raised my hand and said, 'I will sign up.' Denis Hayes said,

'Don't you want to check it with your lawyers first?' and I said, 'No, it is my mission statement. Everything you are saying is what my practice is.'"[10]

To facilitate action, Aveda held all-company morning meetings in which employees were inspired to volunteer and take on environmental responsibilities. "When I asked people to do things that were beyond their routine, such as work on sustainability," Horst said, "I found too often that they just did not do what they said they would do. So I implemented a Project Commitment Form: when a person volunteered to take on a task, the commitment was written down along with the due dates and the form was signed by four other team members with copies distributed throughout the team."[11]

Stonyfield, too, is a founding CERES signatory. While the organization served Stonyfield well for many years, Gary Hirshberg now says that "CERES is no longer part of Stonyfield's daily protocol ever since [CERES] began focusing more on converting large corporations."[12]

The Natural Step Framework

Another, perhaps simpler yet science-based, sustainability management system (and design tool) that has the advantage of not having any specific "must do" requirements is the Natural Step Framework. It was founded in 1989 by Swedish oncologist and karate champion Dr. Karl-Henrik Robèrt in Sweden and popularized by Ray Anderson of Interface Inc. in his book *Mid-Course Correction* and recently by Gil Friend, author of the wonderful book *The Truth About Green Business*. The Natural Step Framework is a sustainability management system with a series of four steps that companies can take to become sustainable.[13] It is so simple yet so effective that hundreds of companies, cities, and communities around the world have implemented it, including most companies in Sweden (like Ikea and Electrolux). In the United States, Nike, Interface Inc., Starbucks, and CH2M Hill employ it as do many other smaller companies and SVN companies such as Mission Research, Portfolio 21, and Benchmark Asset Management. Communities from Santa Monica and Seattle to Madison and Portsmouth, New Hampshire, also employ it. Terry Gips of Sustainability Associates and Paul Hawken—founder of Smith and Hawken and author of *The Ecology of Commerce*—were two of its initial proponents.

Here are the four Natural Step principles:

To become a sustainable society we must eliminate our contribution to:

1. the progressive buildup of substances extracted from the earth's crust (for example, heavy metals and fossil fuels)
2. the progressive buildup of chemicals and compounds produced by society (for example, dioxins, PCBs, and DDT)
3. the progressive physical degradation and destruction of nature and natural processes (for example, unsustainable over-harvesting of forests and paving over critical wildlife habitat); and
4. conditions that undermine people's capacity to meet their basic human needs (for example, unsafe working conditions and not enough pay to live on).[14]

Unlike the CERES Principles, which require a high degree of organizational rigor to implement, the Natural Step process can be effectively implemented with any level of organizational time and resource investment. To do a company-wide Natural Step Framework seminar and action planning session takes a day and a half and costs about \$9,000. Following that, a sustainability team could work out the details of the plan in just a few hours more. To be really effective, the sustainability team should meet monthly for one to two hours. In addition, one person investing two hours per week dealing with e-mails and reports is sufficient.

Whatever approach you use, you can elect to report your sustainability practices and results using the Global Reporting Initiative,[15] which "develops and disseminates globally applicable 'Sustainability Reporting Guidelines' for voluntary use by organizations reporting their economic and sustainability attributes."[16] GRI's latest G3 Sustainability Reporting Guidelines are also available as a free download.

Standards

Standards differ from management systems and frameworks in that they deal with a narrow set of criteria. You may find one or more standards that will advance your mission if you comply with them. To be effective, the criteria in standards need to be SMART—specific, measurable, attainable, relevant, and timely. Attainability is key. If everyone can and does meet a standard, the standard is not doing anything to drive continuous improvement to achieve sustainability. On the other hand, one country's standards body came out with a silly standard for refrigerators that was so rigorous in terms of insulation, seals, and energy efficiency that no product on the market or planned in the future could meet it.

Among the sustainability standards are SVN's Standards of Corporate Social Responsibility.[17] These standards, which are available as a free download, were conceptualized and managed by David, and Joe contributed financing and content for their creation and publication.

Green Seal[18] promulgates environmentally superior consensus-based product standards. It was founded by visionary Rena Shulsky, who cofounded Green Audit with David, and chaired by Denis Hayes. While he was director of standards at Green Seal, David oversaw the development of the first U.S. voluntary standards for energy-efficient lighting, water-efficient fixtures, rerefined engine oil, recycled business paper and sanitary papers, household cleaners, paint, windows and doors, and appliances.

Green Seal's standards are created using an open, transparent process that involves the entire stakeholder community of companies/organizations, trade associations, suppliers, customers/members, public interest groups, regulators, and academicians. Usually a technical committee comprising representatives of these stakeholder groups researches the issues and prepares a draft standard. The standard consists of an introductory statement describing what it covers and what the boundary conditions are, the criteria, labeling instructions, and a glossary with references to other existing standards.

Once initial research is completed, the draft standard is issued with a rationale for each criterion along with measurement parameters. Once the draft standard is published, it undergoes a "purification by fire" process as it is sent to all the identified stakeholder groups and to anyone else who wants it. These stakeholders are invited to send in formal comments. In the revision of the draft standard to create a final version, every comment must be addressed. Often standards undergo multiple revisions until a consensus among the stakeholder groups is reached. The draft U.S. Department of Agriculture (USDA) Standard for Organic Certification, for example, received over 275,000 comments before it was revised and finalized.

Standards are key to all businesses and organizations making continuous improvement. There are thousands of published standards. If sustainability standards don't exist for your area of concentration, consider creating standards that are specific to your operations. Paulette Mae Cole of ABC Home did just that (see chapter 9) in creating the company's "goodwood" standard for sustainably harvested wood used in making furniture.

If you make a standard, your standard can then be nominated to become an ANSI standard and then move on to become an ISO standard.

Summary

To become sustainable, take the steps to convert your vision into action. Many organizations do this directly, such as Stonyfield, which has developed Mission Action Program teams and Problem Solving Groups.

Most organizations follow existing holistic management systems, protocols, and frameworks that comprehensively address all aspects of an organization's impact on the environment. These include ISO 14000, the global standards for environmental management systems; the CERES Principles; and the Natural Step Framework. Other organizations use existing standards to help them piece together the elements necessary to realize their vision. These include SVN's Standards of Corporate Social Responsibility, the USDA organic standard, and Green Seal's product standards.

Organizations that are unable to find existing standards that address their unique products/services, like ABC Home, make their own standards and then "open source" them or promulgate them to become published standards.

Following is a summary of the plan for implementing your sustainability vision:

- Draft and then articulate your sustainability plan, which consists of the steps to realizing your vision.

- Develop or adopt a sustainability management system that seeks excellence, not perfection, and strive for continuous improvement by planning, doing, measuring, and reviewing.

- Develop or adopt sustainability standards and measures of performance that are relevant to your business.

The next chapter provides instructions for three powerful metrics to assess your sustainability and to determine its cost-effectiveness.

Metrics—
If You Can Measure It,
You Can Manage It

This chapter details three powerful analytic tools—the input/output mass balance analysis, life cycle analysis, and break-even analysis. These diagnostic tools help you see what's up with your organization so that you can make changes. The input/output mass balance analysis quantifies your releases to water, emissions to air, and solid waste; the life cycle analysis shows the impact of your product or service from cradle to grave; and the break-even analysis tells you how much savings you will get from environmental improvements or how much you have to decrease costs or increase revenue to pay for environmental improvements.

Input/Output Mass Balance Analysis

Matter cannot be created or destroyed; it can only be changed from one form to another. This basic law of physics and chemistry is the theory behind one of the most powerful tools in sustainability auditing—the input/output mass balance analysis. In simple terms, the weight of the raw materials and manufactured goods you buy plus the water and air you add should equal the weight of products you ship plus the weight of your emissions to air, the weight of garbage and recyclables that leave your facility, and the weight of material you discharge down the drain.

Most large farming operations are now required to do an IOMBA, which tracks the ultimate fate of the nitrogen and phosphorus in the fertilizer and the manure they use to grow their crops.

To see how powerful an IOMBA can be, consider Aveda's story. Dr. Don Stone, an accountant and former business management professor at the University of Massachusetts, led this part of Aveda's audit. He added up the weight of the packaging, the organic ingredients that went into the products, and the water added and then looked at the weight of the products shipped and the concentration of organic ingredients in the products. Don calculated that there were over 1 million pounds of missing organic ingredients—an almost unbelievable discovery, representing about 34 percent of the company's cost of goods.

The big accounting firm that Aveda used had not detected this loss. As far as those accountants were concerned, everything was fine. Aveda bought (very expensive) natural ingredients, mixed them with a lot of water, bottled them, and sold the final packaged products for a very large multiple over the costs of the raw materials, resulting in a large profit. Everyone was happy.

David told Horst Rechelbacher that there were four possibilities as to where the missing 1.2 million pounds of raw organic materials were going. The first possibility was losses of raw material as emissions. The raw materials Aveda bought included a lot of natural, great-smelling volatile organic compounds. During mixing with hot water, the volatiles could, well, volatilize (evaporate). These VOCs could be floating in the air. If this was the case, the problem could be fixed by putting Ping-Pong balls in the vats, installing lids on the batch reactors, or using retorts to condense the volatiles and return them to the vats. David tested the air in the factory for VOCs and multiplied the amount by the fresh air exchange rate. This accounted for only a few thousand pounds of loss on an annual basis.

The second possibility was that the ingredients could be traveling down the drain. During the cleaning process between batches, a significant quantity of product could be accidentally or intentionally discharged. If that was the case, using compressed air to clean tubing or other remediation strategies could control these losses. David reviewed the monthly analysis of the oils, nitrogen, phosphorus, and biological oxygen demand (BOD) of the sewage, and it accounted for only a few thousand pounds of ingredient loss on an annual basis.

The third possibility was that the ingredients to be compounded into products and placed into packaging could have failed quality inspection or been damaged and subsequently thrown away. The contents of the Dumpsters were analyzed and quantified to determine the weight of ingredients thrown away, but this showed that the Dumpsters accounted for only a few thousand pounds of ingredient loss on an annual basis.

As Sherlock Holmes said, "When you have eliminated the impossible, whatever remains, *however improbable*, must be the truth." David told Aveda's audit liaison team that someone was stealing from the company. The plant manager, who was not a fan of the audit in the first place, lost his cool, refuted the findings, and told the other members of the team that the audit was a big waste of time and money.

The owner of the company felt differently. Horst said, "I got a lot out of the audits. I found I had a business that was diverting 34 percent of my raw material. That really raised the flag. I hired a detective agency, which completed the investigation in only one week. The detective said, 'You can drive up to the factory where your material is going. Here is the address.

You can drive up with a station wagon or a delivery van or a truck and pick up whatever you need.'"[1]

The private detective learned that the plant manager had redirected the raw materials to a factory he owned. He was manufacturing products from the raw materials purchased by his employer. Aveda saved millions of dollars by plugging a leak in the supply chain. The audit cost very little in comparison.

Horst added, "Just as the audit was being conducted, Estée Lauder made an offer to buy the company. When I found out how many employees were involved in the rip-off, it broke my heart. It motivated me to get out of the business.

"The whole thing became a great lesson and had a great result because Aveda became the tail that wagged the dog when it was incorporated into Estée Lauder and made Estée Lauder, a much bigger company than Aveda, into a much more environmentally responsible company with a proportionally bigger impact on the world."[2]

PERFORMING AN IOMBA

To perform an IOMBA, you need to try to capture the weight of everything that comes into your facility and everything that leaves your facility.

A powerful tool for enhancing sustainability, the IOMBA is also great for determining shrinkage. At one time Joe owned three coin-operated laundries. Every load of wash requires a predetermined amount of water. If you take total gallons on the water bill and divide it by the amount of water used in each wash, you can tell how many washes were completed. Multiply that by how much is charged per wash and you can see if someone is opening the cash boxes and taking your money. Although Joe didn't realize it at the time, sustainability contributed to profits. His analysis uncovered a theft from the coin boxes and led to the arrest of the thief and to more accurate profits.

Input/output analysis applies to many different enterprises. Another example was in the production of soft drinks at Marty's Soda Mix, owned by Joe. Marty's used an incredible amount of water in making soda. (This was well before the company evolved into a more socially responsible and sustainable business.) Marty's was charged sewage fees based on the amount of water it bought. After completing the input/output mass balance analysis, Joe found that Marty's was being charged for water going into the soft drinks as if the water was going into the sewer drain. Joe installed a separate water meter to track the water in the soft drinks, and the sewage bill decreased by close to 80 percent—another significant savings and contributor to profits.

The more granularity you apply to this exercise, the more accurate your results will become. Whatever you can identify as an input or output, you should quantify. However, you probably will have to do some estimating to complete the mass balance. And the mass balance will rely on inputs you gleaned by performing your sustainability audit. (See resource D to get a structure for your IOMBA.)

For example, weigh your mail and incoming packages a few days per year to make a daily average and multiply by the number of days of mail delivery per year. Or just weigh one of the mail crates, totes, or bags and multiply by the number of containers per day and then by the number of days mail is delivered per year. This gives you a total weight for mail received over the course of the year.

Try to do the input/output analysis for at least your top ten input materials and top ten products. If you use, for example, milk, corn, aluminum, wood, paper, or glass as input material, track the weight of the material through to the output. For example, how much milk comes into the facility? How much milk leaves the facility as product? How much goes down the drain or into the Dumpster?

Measure when you can. Use invoices, bills of lading, and packing slips when you have them. Estimate when you have to.

A sample IOMBA calculation for milk as a raw material is included in resource D.

Finding out where the stuff you buy goes is of critical importance to becoming sustainable and to increasing profits. What action would you take if you knew that 10 percent or even 5 percent of the raw material you buy ends up down the drain, in the Dumpster, in the air, or in someone else's pockets?

If you keep your bills (for purchases as well as for energy, fuel, water, sewage, and waste disposal) accessible and have good records and accounting software, even for a medium-sized manufacturing company, the IOMBA should not take more than one person-week of staff time to prepare.

Life Cycle Analysis

Another comprehensive analysis of the sustainability of your enterprise is the life cycle analysis. The LCA is now the most widely accepted scientific methodology for quantifying a product's or service's environmental impact from cradle to grave or, as green architect, author, and innovator William McDonough describes it, *cradle to cradle*,[3] because ideally a product should have no "grave." It should be able to be recycled into a new product.

David was fortunate to be invited to participate in the evolution of this methodology almost seventeen years ago, working with the EPA and a room full of other scientists. The LCA's premise is to assess and quantify every single impact a product or service has in all stages in its life cycle from preproduction through manufacturing, packaging, and distribution to use and disposal as a function of inputs of energy, water, and material and outputs of releases to water; emissions to air; solids for reuse, recycling, or disposal; ecological considerations; toxicological considerations; and other impacts on humans and the environment.

Key to the efficacy of the LCA are the *boundary conditions* selected—that is, what to include and what not to include in the life cycle analysis. The boundary conditions should be drawn such that the LCA includes all activities where your actions and your money have an impact on the environment.

For example, several life cycle analyses were done to compare cloth diapers (from a diaper service) to disposable diapers. The results initially showed that the disposable diaper was the environmentally superior choice. But an examination of the boundary conditions revealed that the disposable diaper LCA assumed that, as per the manufacturer's instructions, the contents are removed from the disposable diaper and flushed down the toilet prior to disposal, when, in fact, this is almost never done. People toss the diaper with its solid and liquid contents into the garbage. When the LCA was accordingly revised, it showed that the diaper service cloth diaper was the superior choice.

For companies in the dairy business, such as Ben & Jerry's and Stonyfield Farm, several published LCAs have shown that over 90 percent of the adverse impact of milk products in terms of carbon and other polluting emissions to air and releases to water is on the farm. If you are a milk product manufacturer and you don't have boundary conditions to account for these on-farm life cycle impacts, your LCA is meaningless.

Gary Hirshberg of Stonyfield agrees. "What we do to green the company inside, even if we completely eliminated our internal environmental footprint, still has a minimal impact on our overall environmental footprint. The biggest environmental issue is the cows on the farm. Conventional factory farms have the biggest impact. Feedlot organic farms [where the cows are confined but fed organic feed] have a lower impact. Organic family farms where the cows are pasture fed have the lowest impact. To lower it even more, we have implemented our Greener Cow program to address cows' enteric emissions [burps] of methane. As part of that, we just completed a six-month study where we took cows off corn and soy and put them on flax, and we got up to a 19 percent decrease in methane emissions. Methane is the second most impactful greenhouse gas with over twenty times the impact of carbon dioxide per molecule. Not only was there a precipitous drop in emissions, but there also was a huge improvement in omega-3."[4]

Stonyfield's second biggest impact is packaging. After the University of Michigan's Center for Sustainable Systems did an LCA on Stonyfield's packaging, the company implemented the suggestions and reduced its packaging impact by 12 percent in one year.

In another case, life cycle analyses revealed that the edible chelating agent ethylenediaminetetraacetic acid (EDTA) contained in detergents, cold cuts, and mayonnaise, went right through the wastewater treatment plants unmodified. When it was discharged into rivers and streams that had previously been contaminated with heavy metals, the EDTA pulled the heavy metals out of the sediments and resuspended them in the water column, repolluting the rivers with heavy metals.

If you have to err in the precision of your LCA boundary conditions, err on the conservative side—assume the boundary conditions are greater than you imagine. This is part of the basis of the Precautionary Principle, which is required by law in some places. The Precautionary Principle requires that an action or substance be proved safe before you do it or use it.

Make sure that your purchases are on the correct side of the boundary when doing your LCA. Your purchasing decisions have a profound impact on the planet. You'll find more on purchasing considerations in chapter 9.

LCAs provide powerful and often-unanticipated insights into the impact of a company's products and services. The LCA aspect of the Aveda audit, for example, revealed that because of the company's choice to source ingredients entirely from plants, which included the planting and maintenance of various trees from which the ingredients were sustainably harvested, Aveda actually sequestered more carbon dioxide annually than it produced, including the emissions of the fuel used to run its facilities and transport its products. Aveda had no net carbon footprint and actually was a net oxygen producer.

Horst Rechelbacher said, "The LCA showed that every time a client picks up a bottle of our shampoo they are greening the planet. Hearing that was a great moment for me."[5]

Another company that got good news from an LCA was Motherwear, which manufactures garments that allow women to breast-feed discretely. Jody Wright, Motherwear's president, said, "My major goal in developing Motherwear was to support mothers to nurse their babies. Breast-feeding has a profound impact on the health and happiness of families and especially newly developing human beings."[6] For Jody, the great environmental impact of breast-feeding—reduction in transportation, animal feed, waste, carbon monoxide, feeding supplies, and so on—is simply frosting on the cake.

By producing garments that empowered women to breast-feed and because of Motherwear's communications outreach, Jody estimates that the company has touched 1 million women. The average Motherwear customer breast-fed her child for 16 months compared to 2.3 months for the average American mother. The company's LCA showed that for the 1 million women Motherwear touched, 58 million pounds of steel was saved (from infant formula cans), 15 million pounds of fiber was saved (from paper labels on the cans, boxes for the cans, and tampons because breast-feeding delays the onset of menstruation). In addition, 1 billion pounds of cow milk was not produced and fed to infants. This saved 625 million gallons of water, 270,000 pounds of herbicides, 80,000 pounds of insecticides, and 12 million pounds of synthetic fertilizer, as well as 15 million gallons of oil, which would have produced 325 million pounds of carbon dioxide needing 83,000 acres of forest to absorb.

One of the challenges of LCAs is that the results sometimes seem like apples and oranges. For example, what is worse—one manufacturing process that produces 5 million pounds of biological oxygen demand, another that produces 500 pounds of mercury, or another that produces 5 curies of plutonium?

There is a way to convert from apples and oranges to apples and apples so that you can compare alternatives. In fact, you do it all the time when you use money. Money has become the supreme arbiter of value. Every activity can be scored in terms of money.

For example, the Tellus Institute in Boston performed a life cycle analysis of packaging materials under a contract from EPA, the New Jersey Department of Environmental Quality, and some industry trade associations. After Tellus inventoried and quantified all of the inputs, environmental releases, and impacts, it "monetized" the environmental impacts by assigning costs for environmental remediation. The dollar figures effectively indicated what it would cost, on a per-ton basis, to eliminate all of the environmental problems created by the packaging.

LCAs are complex and can involve hundreds of thousands of calculations. You can hire professionals whose specialty is preparing LCAs. These LCAs can cost up to $250,000 or more. However, there is still value in doing one yourself.

Resource E includes a blank Life Cycle Analysis Matrix and an example of a completed one. We recommend that you complete one for every company and new product, process, or service you are contemplating introducing and for your existing main products, processes, and services. Complete an LCA Matrix at least qualitatively, if not quantitatively, to the best of your ability and available resources. Even the most expensive, professionally prepared LCAs begin with the completion of an LCA Matrix.

To simplify the process and make it easier to understand, after you write a few qualitative words in every box, color code each box in the matrix: red for the most severe environmental impacts, yellow for a marginal impact, or green for no negative impact. Every impact for each company, product, or service should fit into at least one category on the matrix.

As part of Walmart's new Sustainability Index,[7] not only is the company requiring its vendors to fill out vendor questionnaires (see chapter 9), but it is also requiring LCAs to be done on all of its products by 2012, and these LCAs will all be open sourced and available to everyone. To this end the company has helped create the Sustainability Consortium,[8] an organization of manufacturing companies working with Walmart and the University of Arkansas and Arizona State University.

A large number of LCAs are already open sourced and available. The United Nations Environment Program in conjunction with the Society for Environmental Toxicology and Chemistry (UNEP-SETAC) has created an International Life Cycle Partnership, known as the Life Cycle Initiative,[9] from which you can access many completed LCAs for various products, processes, and services.

EPA has a life cycle assessment resource[10] from which you can access LCA information. Included in it is a summary of global life cycle inventory data resources. The National Renewable Energy Laboratory has LCAs in seventy-three different product categories.[11] If your product or service is not there, you can combine many of these seventy-three to recreate your product.

Break-Even Analysis

A comprehensive understanding of your financial statement is an integral component of sustainability. As our friend Ben Cohen is fond of saying, "A business can be successful as a business and unsuccessful as a force for social change, but it cannot be unsuccessful as a business and successful as a force for social change."

Every small and medium-sized business must have adequate financial accounting controls, and the owner or manager must review these numbers on a regular basis. Although our concentration has been on nonfinancial considerations for sustainability, we strongly urge you to have a deep-rooted understanding of your past financial performance, present position, and future budget projections.

Performing a break-even analysis will provide you with the tools you need to make an informed decision on whether a sustainability cost will have a positive return on investment (ROI).

To prepare a break-even analysis, you have to look at every line item in your profit and loss (P&L) statement and ask the question, "What are the fixed expenses that I will incur even if I don't sell a single product or service?" Put those items in the fixed expenses column.

For those items that you have to buy and replace only if you are actually selling product, put those items under variable cost. Sometimes an item will be split between fixed expenses and variable cost. Then add up the variable costs and the fixed expenses. The total variable cost is then divided by the net sales, producing the variable cost percentage. Subtracting this percentage from 100 percent yields the profit projector. When you divide the total fixed expenses by the profit projector, the result is the company's break-even point.

You can do this exercise whether your P&L is very detailed with many lines or not very detailed at all. The more detail, the more accurate your break-even analysis will be, but either way this will give you a very powerful insight into your business and the bottom-line impact of implementing sustainability programs.

In the example below, the company manufactures and sells devices for reducing electrical consumption for lighting. It buys components, trying to order on a just-in-time basis, and assembles them. The company's P&L shows its net sales as $3,704,000 with a $596,100 net profit. The calculations result in total variable costs of $2,077,375 and fixed expenses of $1,030,525.

To calculate the break-even point, first divide the total variable costs by the net sales. The result is approximately 56.1% ($2,077,375/ $3,704,000).

Next, determine the profit projector by subtracting the above from 100%. The result is 43.9% (100% – 56.1%).

Now divide the total fixed expenses by the profit projector to get the break-even point. The result is $2,346,616 ($1,030,525/43.9%).

The break-even point is the amount of net sales needed to break even. Sales above this number mean you profit and below this number mean you lose money.

Imagine that our hypothetical company opens the door on the first day of the fiscal year. And when someone walks in and buys an item for $1 (hooray), $0.56 of that dollar goes to cover the cost of goods, the labor associated with the item's assembly, the incremental portion of utilities and office supplies necessary to fulfill that sale, and taxes. That leaves $0.44, but this is not profit. The company still has its fixed expenses of $1,030,525 to pay off. The entire $0.44 goes toward paying off the $1,030,525.

Another item is sold for $1. Another $0.56 is spent in filling the order, leaving another $0.44 to pay off the fixed expenses.

At the break-even point, the fixed expenses are all paid off and after the $0.56 per dollar is taken out to cover the variable costs, the remaining $0.44 is profit.

How much profit does the company make if it has sales of $1,000,000 over the break-even point? It makes $440,000 ($1,000,000 × 44%). At $2,000,000 over break even, it makes $880,000 ($2,000,000 × 44%). If it is $500,000 under break even, the company loses $220,000 ($500,000 × 44%).

If, through preventing the disposal of a raw material, using waste as a raw material, reusing packaging material, or increasing energy efficiency, the company is able to lower its variable costs by 1%, what impact would that have on its break-even point and profits?

To find out, multiply the variable costs by 99% (100% − 1%), which yields $2,056,601. The variable cost percent of net sales becomes 55.5% ($2,056,601/$3,704,000). The new profit projector becomes 44.5% (100% − 55.5%). Calculate the new break-even point by dividing the fixed expenses by the new profit projector ($1,030,525/44.5%). The result is $2,317,025, which is $29,591 less than the previous break-even point.

The net profit under this new break even is $616,874 ($3,704,000 − $1,030,525 − $2,056,601), a 3.5% increase in profit. For this model company, a 1% decrease in variable cost produces a 3.5% increase in profit. For many companies we have worked with, a 1% reduction in variable costs has produced an increase in profit by 100% or more.

Now, let's say the company wants to spend $1,000 to make a fixed expense improvement in its operations by installing energy-efficient lighting, water-efficient fixtures, or renewable energy systems or by sending several employees to a course on diversity or green marketing. How much more sales would it have to get to pay for the $1,000 fixed expense? Divide the fixed expense by the profit projector ($1,000/43.9%) to get $2,277.

Even for large capital equipment, like a fuel-efficient furnace, a wind machine, or solar panels, the specific new fixed expense would manifest itself on the P&L as annual depreciation and, if the item is financed, annual interest.

This break-even analysis becomes a very powerful tool in gauging the cost-effectiveness of everything you do to make your company more sustainable. The break-even analysis can also be done on companies that are losing money to see what sales they need to do to break even.

The break-even analysis does not take into consideration capital and liquidity. However, it provides a tool for financiers (banks, lending institutions, investors, etc.) to evaluate the long-term prospects of an enterprise. You can find out more about the break-even analysis on the Web site associated with this book.[12]

Summary

The three metrics outlined in this chapter help to uncover theft and waste possibilities, disclose life cycle environmental impact, and tighten up financial management. The sustainable business moves beyond the financial statement and attempts to uncover all the environmental exposures related to the organization's activities.

Three powerful sustainability tools can help you achieve this goal:

- The input/output mass balance analysis quantifies what you use and what you produce and maps where everything you use and produce goes.

- The life cycle analysis helps you uncover the impact of your products or services from cradle to grave.

- The break-even analysis helps you calculate what the financial upside or downside is for any sustainability capital expenditure or increase or decrease in material or operating costs.

With audits and life cycle, mass balance and break-even analyses, you have a great picture of where you are and a great launch point to go forward. The next chapter deals with using green design to minimize your footprint and maximize your opportunities.

Design—
Making It Sustainable
from the Start

The best way to get green is to design green. Every company or enterprise is constantly involved in design. Organizations design innovative products and services and innovative ways to make existing products and to perform existing and new tasks. So green design is a common entry point for companies seeking to become sustainable. This chapter provides guidance on sustainable green design of products and services.

It turns out that proactive green design is much more cost-effective than reactive solutions to environmental challenges. The design Rule of Tens states that if it costs $10 to come up with design criteria, it costs $100 for the actual design, $1,000 for the prototype, $10,000 for the preproduction run, $100,000 to produce the product, and $1 million to recall it after a flaw is discovered that could have been addressed in the $10 design phase.

Review Your LCA

In chapter 4 we discussed the life cycle analysis. The first rule in sustainable design is to review all of the LCA categories. To design a more sustainable product, ask and answer the question, "What improvements can be designed into the product in the preproduction, manufacturing, packaging, distribution, use, and disposal phases as a function of inputs of energy, water, and material, and outputs of emissions to air, releases to water and solid waste, and impacts on human health and ecology?" If you completed an LCA matrix (see resource E), the boxes that are highlighted in red represent the greatest environmental impact. These are the areas to focus on in your green design efforts for the next product iteration.

Qteros is an example of a start-up company that came into existence from intentional green design. Jef Sharp, along with his partners in a string of successful businesses, decided

> We wanted to start a new business, but this time we wanted to do a business for the planet. We created criteria for starting green companies that can help the world. We then looked at a lot of opportunities including fuel cells, ethanol fuel injection, energy conservation, solar energy, and green plastics, and we settled on the Q microbe discovered by Dr. Sue Leschine of the University of Massachusetts at Amherst. She found a microbe near the Quabbin Reservoir in Massachusetts that ate cellulose and produced a very small amount of ethanol.
>
> From the beginning I believed that Sue's discovery would be a home run. However, had I seen all the trials and tribulations that we would have to go through, I probably would not have even started. We had read that Richard Branson of Virgin Airlines, Records, and Megastores had set up a Green Fuels Fund. We were just three guys in a garage, but we had the chutzpah to make the call, and before you know it, we were on a plane to London and then had terms for a deal from him. Because

Branson took us seriously, so did others, and we actually ending up turning down Branson for a better deal.

The better deal eventually resulted in a total of $25 million in funding from BP, Soros Management Fund, Venrock (the "rock" part of this firm's name comes from the Rockefeller origins of the fund), and Battery Ventures. This paid for development resulting in progress on evolving the Q microbe without use of genetic engineering from its original 0.2 gram of ethanol per liter to over 4 grams per liter, which is the thermodynamic break-even point of more energy out than in.[1]

Jef and his partners started with the concept of using a life cycle approach and designing a green business and now have a technology that can convert switch grass, corn stover, wood waste, and now even the solids in sewage into a renewable energy liquid transportation fuel with a carbon footprint 90–95 percent better than gasoline, according to Argonne National Laboratories' life cycle analysis.

Look at Your Current Process

The second rule to green design improvements is examining every current process step and asking the question, "Why is it done this way, and is there a better way to do it?"

David worked with a manufacturer of compact fluorescent lights (CFLs). Due to regulations, the company had to eliminate a fluorochlorinated solvent it used to clean metal parts after they were stamped out from cold rolled steel. The parts were cleaned so that they could be electroplated first with copper, then with nickel, and finally with chrome for corrosion protection. Try as it might, every new cleaning solvent the company used failed to remove all the rust from the edges of the metal stamped parts. With rusty edges the electroplating could not produce a corrosion-proof seal. Ultimately the company had to give up and use expensive stainless steel instead of cold rolled steel, which was eight times cheaper. But because the parts did not have to be cleaned after stamping and then have three successive electroplating coatings, the whole product ended up being 30 percent cheaper.

When the foreman in charge of that section of the manufacturing line was asked why the parts were ever made with cold rolled steel that needed to be cleaned and have multiple coats of electroplating, he said, "That's the way the previous foreman showed me how to do it when I first got here." The initial design decision was never reexamined.

Challenge any and all preexisting paradigms and beliefs. Ask, "Why is this product made from this material and made in this way?" At the product's genesis, there might have been a sale or promotion on a component or ingredient. The component may be part of the design just because the original purchasing agent's sister-in-law's company was selling the material or component. A better material may have been recently developed. Look at the function of the component or material and ask, "What is the best, greenest, most cost-effective way to fulfill this function?"

This type of self-analysis can yield some very unexpected results. Jeffrey Hollender, cofounder of Seventh Generation, which manufactures a full line of household cleaning products, said, "We assumed our biggest impact was related to the manufacture of our products—the waste created by making the products. However, our biggest impact was finding that our products were designed to work in hot water, and we found that the impact of heating the water was greater than any impact from manufacturing. So we reformulated our products to work as well in cold water as in warm water."[2]

Don't Choose the Lesser of Two Evils

It's really easy to design green products. It becomes difficult when you try to design green products that people can actually afford. While there is a market for the true-blue greens, who always buy products that are better for the environment, most people will buy a green product only if it is comparable in price and quality with other products. The challenge, therefore, is not to design green products but to design green products that are cost-effective.

As you move through the green design process, you often will be faced with choosing the lesser of two evils. Green design rule number three is, when you get to that juncture of choosing between the lesser of two evils, the correct answer is "None of the above." The challenge is to rethink the design until you come to a solution that is truly green and cost-effective. We have never had the experience where the green, cost-effective answer was perpetually elusive. It just may take longer to come up with it.

Find a Better Way to Meet the Purpose

Rule number four is to ask, "What is the purpose of the product, and can the purpose be met using a greener and more cost-effective way?" If, for example, you are in the business of making drill bits, it is important to realize that nobody really wants a ¼-inch drill bit. What the customer really wants is a ¼-inch hole. Think of the best, greenest, and cheapest way you can deliver the result that the customer wants.

Many companies have reinvented themselves by asking this question "What is the purpose of the product or service we have been providing, and can we do it better, greener, cheaper?" For example, Interface Inc. sells modular carpeting, mostly for industrial applications. If a section of carpeting wears out, instead of getting new carpeting, the customer can replace just the worn-out piece, saving money and resources. This creates customer loyalty. The people at Interface Inc. see themselves not in the business of selling carpeting but in the business of providing a floor covering service.

How would you make your product and packaging different if you and not your customer retained ownership of the product? For example, customers don't need lubricating oil; they need lubrication. What if you provided lubrication services to your customers instead of just selling them oil? That is essentially what Safety-Kleen does.

Consider renting your product instead of selling it. One publisher, Cengage Learning, rents textbooks to students for 40 percent to 70 percent of the retail price. In a close-to-perfect example of creating the quintessential sustainable enterprise, Better World Books designed a greener way of providing books to its customers. Better World Books is a for-profit social enterprise that collects used books from colleges and libraries and sells them online at costs significantly less than the cost of new books. It's saving trees and landfill space and, now highly profitable, also raising money for literacy initiatives worldwide.

Many manufacturing companies design in "planned obsolescence." They intentionally design an inferior product so that the product will break just after the warranty runs out. Other companies do the opposite. Tilley Hat, Pelican Case, and Coach Leather provide their customers with lifetime guarantees. Tilley boasts that an elephant ate one of its hats three times. Each time it was recovered from the elephant's dung, washed, and worn again. Designing a product to be durable is key to successful green design.

One other very important point in green design is efficacy. In addition to the product having a minimal environmental footprint, it also has to do its job. One manufacturer of "green" cleaning products claimed that its products had the lowest environmental footprint of all competing products. That was true on a pound-per-pound basis. What was also true was that in efficacy tests conducted by Green Seal, water outperformed the products as a cleaning agent. When designing a sustainable product, make sure that it does the job it is supposed to do and is the best product in its category.

Design to Sustainability Product Standards

While Green Seal produced the first set of sustainability product standards in this country, a large number of standards now exist. When designing a product, ensure that your product handily meets all the appropriate sustainability and efficacy criteria. When a standard has a quantified limit—for example, for mercury in a CFL, VOCs in water-based paint, or lead and hexavalent chromium in ink—be aware that the next version of the standard is likely to have even lower limits than the current published thresholds, and design accordingly.

Those who adopt voluntary standards that surpass existing regulations will be much farther ahead of the competition and have a distinct competitive advantage. The sustainability standard from another country may shed light on the product category's sustainability or regulatory future. For example, while no laws address the specific issue in the United States, all nail polish sold in Europe must be phthalate free. Sweden had rigorous standards for electromagnetic radiation (EMR) emanating from a computer monitor that have since been adopted as voluntary global manufacturing standards. During your green design phase, consult existing sustainability standards from this country and other countries. Most of them are in English. The "Notes and Resources" section in the back of the book provides a list of several sustainability standard-setting organizations.[3]

Some standards show trends—for example, for CFLs, no more than 25 milligrams (mg) of mercury is allowed until 2010, then 5 mg of mercury after that. Follow the trend in your design work. In this specific case, the writing on the wall is clear: try to use zero mercury in your product.

If no green product standard exists for your product category, make one up. You can read about ABC Home's experience in developing its own standards in chapter 9.

Some places have also enacted extended product responsibility (EPR) laws or protocols based on the concept that a manufacturer's responsibility for a product extends beyond the time of sale. This view incorporates a cradle-to-the-grave conception of products and relieves consumers and local governments from the costs of cleanup and dangerous materials.[4] For example, the German Green Dot program[5] lets manufacturers voluntarily provide a recycling infrastructure for their product packaging. If the Green Dot appears on a product package, the consumer knows that the manufacturer has effectively prepaid for the item to be recycled.

Consider implementing EPR criteria into your next product design. Some companies have even started designing their products so that the product can be disassembled with the components refurbished and sold as reconditioned used parts.

When All Else Fails, Cheat

Copy other brilliant green designers. We happen to know the best one, and fortunately, none of her designs have intellectual property protections—Mother Nature. In the multibillion years of life on this planet, every design permutation and combination has been tried. In the millions of different animals, plants, and fungal and microbial species, every imaginable and unimaginable trick and trait has been tried and either perfected or discarded. Flight, light without heat, waterproof superglues, armor, air conditioning, poisons—all have been done sustainably. For example, the configurations of every type of aircraft— jet fighters, bombers, cargo planes, reconnaissance vehicles, gliders—are virtually identical in design and function to those of different types of birds. Biomimicry is the science of how one organism mimics another and is the science of mimicking biology to design better products.

Our favorite pioneer of biomimicry is Sara Little Turnbull, director of the Process of Change, Innovation, and Design Laboratory at Stanford University's Graduate School of Business. She was editor of *House Beautiful* in the 1940s and 1950s. She also invented Pyrex cookware for Corning and the suits worn by the astronauts on the lunar landings. (By the way, the suits were made of textured soy protein and were edible.) She designed pot handles inspired by watching cheetahs catch and hold onto prey at 70 miles per hour during her trips to Africa. She invented 3M's antipollution masks made from non-woven fiber. Her green design process is simple: she observes and copies nature.

Author, architect, and visionary William McDonough led the greening of the White House under President Bill Clinton. He was also the innovator of the EcoMart—Walmart's first attempt at sustainable building design for its Livermore, Kansas, facility. In the course of the green design phase, Bill essentially invented a new type of superinsulated window that transmits light but not heat. One of the candidate manufacturers multiplied the number of windows needed by the number of

Walmart stores and responded, "We'll make this window if we can sell it to all the Walmart stores." Bill replied that the manufacturer could have the order only if it provided the window not just to Walmart but to all its customers.

Bill prepared comprehensive sustainable design principles when creating the 2000 Hannover World's Fair in Germany.[6] These principles are a powerful green design tool, and we recommend you review them before embarking on your green design efforts.

Summary

This chapter takes what we learned in chapter 4 on life cycle analysis and integrates those considerations into designing new products and redesigning products already in use. Your goal is to challenge any and all preexisting manufacturing techniques and raw materials usage with an eye toward sustainability. Countless examples demonstrate that you will find a better solution and business opportunities with totally unexpected conclusions. Jeffrey Hollender of Seventh Generation realized that the greatest impact of his household cleaning products came from heating the water to use the products, not the product themselves. Nature is the finest example of sustainability, and many standards and design tools copy nature. You can too.

The easiest and most cost-effective way to be green is to design green. When designing,

- Use a life cycle approach to green design.
- Always ask, "Why is it done this way, and is there a better way to do it?"
- Never choose between the lesser of two evils.
- Ask, "What is the purpose of the product, and can the purpose be met using a greener and more cost-effective way?"

- Design to existing and anticipated environmental standards.
- Employ biomimicry—copy nature.
- Use existing sustainable design tools.

One aspect of green design is green facility design. The next chapter discusses a key component of every enterprise's sustainability profile—its workplace.

Facility—
Making Your Workplace Green

Both "ecology" and "economy" have their roots in the Greek word *oikos*, meaning "home." This chapter deals with the ecology and economy of your enterprise's home and how to make your enterprise's facility more sustainable. If you have a virtual business, then your business's home is your home. Your business's home and the energy to maintain it can be the biggest environmental burden your enterprise causes or they can have a zero net impact if you make the right choices in terms of construction materials, energy efficiency, water conservation, and indoor environmental quality. Green building protocols can help you address all these issues.

Construction Materials

The ultimate sustainable construction materials were employed in renovating the College Hall at New College, Oxford, built in 1386. After five hundred years, the oak beams supporting the ceiling started to decay and needed replacing. Oak trees take five hundred years to produce such massive beams, so they are not easy to source and would be expensive if you could find them. After many years of searching, replacements were discovered in two separate stands of oak trees in Buckinghamshire. It turned out both forests were owned by Oxford College. Presumably, the College Hall builders in 1386 sustainably planned for the ceiling's replacement. The giant oaks were cut down and the old beams replaced.

As the Chinese proverb goes, "The best time to plant a tree is twenty [or more] years ago. The second best time is today."

Wood can be a wonderful, sustainable material to build with. It meets all the green design criteria and then some in that it is produced by nature and, when it has completed its intended use, it can be recycled, composted, or burned as a source of energy with no carbon footprint. Until then it represents a form of carbon sequestration that helps to mitigate global warming.

One of the problems with wood is that in recent years, it has been a victim of unsustainable harvesting methods. Old growth forests have been clear-cut. By clear-cutting, huge tracts of land are denuded of all life—not just the trees but also the animals that depend on them. Without trees to hold the soil down, these clear-cut areas are quickly eroded by wind and rain, and the soil (a complex ecosystem containing a trove of nutrients) is washed away. It can take hundreds, even thousands, of years for the soil to replace itself and support a forest of equal biomass. The nutrients that were washed away in turn overnutrify and silt up the receiving streams, rivers, and lakes, causing eutrophication, a bloom of aquatic plants that use up all the dissolved oxygen, resulting in death to the fish. While some laws regulate clear-cutting and forestry management, they are neither comprehensive nor adequate.

In the 1990s the Forest Stewardship Council (FSC)[1] began the process of setting standards for sustainably harvesting wood. Today, you can buy FSC-certified hardwood. This certification applies to sustainable harvesting of forests as well as tree plantations for construction materials, pulp (paper), and other uses.

Contrary to popular belief, trees like the redwoods are not protected species. Stands of redwoods on private land, even if they are over a thousand years old, can still be cut down and cause grievous environmental problems. To address this, an organization called Old Growth Again (now Forever Redwood)[2] was created. It developed a technology to take clear-cut redwood stands and immediately plant new redwood trees. It prevents erosion by laying the branches and debris left after clear-cutting perpendicular to the downhill slope, and new redwood trees are planted under faster growing fir trees, which are harvested in five years, providing the cash flow to make this sustainable forestry method profitable. Old Growth Again makes outdoor furniture from the old, discarded decay-resistant redwood stumps that have been lying around these clear-cut forests for decades.

A novel sustainable woodlike building material comes from SVN member Robert Hendrikson, who previously successfully pioneered the commercial farming of algae. His new company, Bamboo Sun[3], makes prefabricated buildings entirely out of sustainable bamboo, which is a grass.

John Schaeffer, founder and president of Real Goods and the Solar Living Institute, has experimented with renovating and creating structures that are sustainable, are made from sustainable materials (like bales of hay and mud), and are either energy efficient or powered by renewable energy (hydro-power, wind power, and photovoltaics [PV]). The Solar Living Institute[4] is a place to see them, and Real Goods[5] sells the plans and hardware.

Energy Efficiency

Passive solar construction was first described by Plato. He advised people to build homes with south-facing porticos (roof overhangs) so that when the sun is high in the sky during the hot summer months, the sun hits the portico, keeping the room interior shaded and cooler, and when the sun is low in the sky in the winter, the sunlight enters the home from below the portico, warming the house.

This is pretty much the technology behind passive solar buildings today. Enhancements include superinsulated structures with large south-facing windows and small or no north-facing windows. To further enhance efficiency, well-insulated windows are used. Generally, these consist of at least two panes of glass with a sealed air space in between. The glazing material has a low-emissivity film coating, making it transparent to visible light but opaque to infrared light (heat) so that the heat remains outside. Enhancements of the coating include materials like vanadium pentoxide, which acts as a thermal diode, letting the infrared heat energy escape when the weather is warm and retaining the heat when it is cold.

Another feature of passive solar construction is thermal mass. Heat is stored in massive amounts of material (like water, rocks, or even materials, like Glauber's salt, which changes from solid to liquid and back) and is released slowly and passively. A large thermal mass also provides for thermal buffering—keeping a place at a constant temperature longer, despite changes in temperature outside.

Water provides a great and inexpensive thermal mass. A ton of water will store the heat of approximately ⅓ gallon of oil per day. In New England, for example, with a 180-day heating cycle, at $2.50 per gallon of heating oil, that can mean about $150 per heating season of heat held onto and not lost per ton of thermal mass.

Energy is an important part of what makes for a sustainable structure or facility, but it is by no means all. Energy is dealt with extensively in chapter 7. Water conservation is another important aspect of a facility's environmental footprint.

Water Conservation

At the Longfellow Clubs, the men's bathrooms all have water-less toilets. This has reduced flushing in the men's rooms by 80 percent and saves 300,000 gallons of water per year. Another major use of water in health clubs is for showering. David worked in the 1990s on setting standards for water-efficient fix-tures such as showerheads (2.5 gallons per minute [gpm]) and faucets (0.5 gpm), and most places now have these standards enacted into law, but many water-conserving showerheads just don't provide the satisfaction that the old 5.5 gpm shower-heads did. Longfellow Clubs' Laury Hammel noted, "The holy grail of water and energy conservation at health clubs is showerheads—a showerhead that is under 2 gpm that feels like a shower and not a drip. We found two showerheads that do the job. Our showers are running a full day every twenty-four hours times sixty showers. They used to be 4 gpm and now they are 2 gpm. We have saved tons of water and energy by putting in aerators in the faucets as well."[6]

A building's landscaped grounds can waste a huge amount of water. Many thoughtful planners are landscaping facilities so that they use only indigenous plants that thrive on the ambi-ent rainfall. Others are using a technique called xeriscaping, which entails planting drought-tolerant plants and using pre-cise watering techniques, such as subsurface drip-irrigation tubes that meter water and apply it at specific times.

In places like the Northeast and Northwest, 2,000 square feet of rooftop or parking lot can collect about 50,000 gallons of water per year. Most facilities send the rainwater that lands on the roof and grounds to the municipal wastewater treatment facility, where it costs about the same to treat as sewage. Excess rainwater falling on the roof and not used for a rooftop garden can be collected, run through a sand filter, and stored. This gray (nonpotable) water can be used for applications like flushing toilets, washing clothes and floors, and watering plants and lawns. The water stored in this tank can also be used for thermal mass to reduce the amount of energy needed for heating and cooling.

Indoor Environmental Quality

Make sure that your facility takes in enough fresh air for the number of people that work there. Stonyfield had a relatively high absenteeism rate in its accounting department. During an audit, David found elevated levels of CO_2 in the accounting offices. He traced the problem to the fact that one cold winter, to address complaints, the building maintenance person closed the fresh air intake on the heating system for that section of the building. The valve was opened and absenteeism immediately dropped. Elevated CO_2 levels due to poor fresh air intake are common in a large portion of the facilities that David has tested.

Tommy Boy Entertainment was another company with indoor air pollution. It was the premier hip-hop music company whose hit labels included Queen Latifah, Coolio, Everlast, RuPaul, and many others. It had a very high rate of employee stress, headaches, and absenteeism. But management was not alarmed by these high rates since the company was located in New York City and record production is a traditionally high-stress industry.

Tom Silverman, Tommy Boy's president, said, "I thought we would do a great thing for our employees to address this, so I brought in a flotation tank, a yoga room, and in-company massage therapists. We also made people take a break each day to stop work and stop looking at their computer monitors, hoping they would meditate. Most ended up just reading the newspaper. We also had an eco-audit that looked at electromagnetic radiation and indoor air quality. At that time the World Trade Center was still standing, and its dish antennas were aimed right at us. Fortunately, the testing showed no elevated levels of electromagnetic radiation. However, when we tested the air for indoor air pollutants, we discovered a high rate of formaldehyde—lower than legal limits but higher than voluntary published standards and at a rate that, based on published reports, predicted the level of stress, headache, and absenteeism. The eco-auditors first looked for a source of the formaldehyde and found over 100 items in the offices that were potential formaldehyde outgassing agents, including Formica, carpeting, office module panels, and many other items."[7]

It was not practical to remove all the items, so the company needed another way to deal with the elevated formaldehyde levels. Indoor plants such as philodendron and spider plants are known to sequester formaldehyde, so plants were put wherever lighting would support their healthy growth, but there were not enough well-lit locations for plants alone to fix the problem. Another way to deal with formaldehyde or other indoor air pollutants in the work environment is to exchange the air with greater frequency—bring in more fresh air. ASHRAE (American Society of Heating, Refrigerating, and Air-Conditioning Engineers) Standard 62 for fresh air exchange suggests ventilation of 20 cubic feet per minute of fresh air per person in a facility. During the eco-audit, Tom told David that he had invested in an air-handling system that actually brought in fresh air at a rate of five times the ASHRAE standard and had spent a fortune on the equipment.

After a review of the blueprints, David put a wind sock on the air intake to make sure it was up to the specs. Surprisingly, the fresh air exchange rate was six times *worse* than the ASHRAE standard, not five times better. When David and Tom contacted the contractor (one of the biggest heating, ventilating, and air-conditioning [HVAC] contractors in the world) and explained the discrepancy, the representative quickly apologized, and the company took out the system and installed the correct system. One can only guess at how many facilities have air-handling systems that have not met the specifications ordered. David notes that about half of the companies he has audited have fresh air exchange rates lower than the ASHRAE standard.

When you contract for a building, it is easy to check if you got the five floors you paid for, the marble tile in the lobby you specified, 10-foot-high ceilings, lighting that illuminates the room you are in, and an HVAC system that keeps the place warm in winter and cool in summer. You also need to validate the specifications that you can't verify with your five senses. Check the fresh air exchange and indoor air quality. Check the quality of the well or municipal water supply (sometimes pipes leach the strangest things) as well as the water quality coming off a filtration or reverse osmosis unit. Check the electromagnetic frequencies at all the workstations and other parameters that impact human health and comfort—and therefore profitability. If a building is sick, the inhabitants will get sick. A healthy building creates the atmosphere for a healthy work environment.

Very little attention is paid to electromagnetic radiation in the work environment. Ten years ago, David found lots of companies with computer monitors, microwave ovens, and cell phones that had excessively high levels of EMR, but since then the multinational manufacturers have adopted voluntary international standards for EMR exposure and we see less of it from these devices now. In old buildings with antiquated or exotic wiring systems and electric space heaters, high levels of EMR are still found. At Mal Warwick Associates, the audit found elevated levels of electromagnetic radiation in a few of the senior managers' offices. This was addressed by switching space around and using these former executive offices for storage, so people have less exposure to the elevated levels of radiation.

A man whose two sons worked with him as the senior management team owned another company David worked with. The man and his sons worked together in one large room within a machine shop and office complex in Jamaica, New York. They had lathes, screw machines, and two- and three-axis metal carving machines and computer numerically controlled machines for making precision metal parts. The father had such an unpleasant disposition that he dissolved away the lining of his stomach with ulcers. One son was so unhappy that he hanged himself from the ceiling in an unsuccessful suicide attempt. The other son was equally miserable.

What was causing this misery? To keep cool in their office, they had installed a ceiling fan with blades that rotated below the drop ceiling fluorescent lights. Fluorescent lights pulse at 60 cycles per second. The fan blades created a stroboscopic effect with the ceiling lighting at frequencies known to cause irritability. The three men actually became cheery when the ceiling fan was removed. You can buy electronic (versus magnetic) fluorescent ballasts that bump the frequency up to 20,000 cycles per second, which avoids negative human behavioral effects. Or just don't put a fan between you and your fluorescent lamps.

Similar to the case above, another company David worked with built a new restaurant that initially enjoyed instant success. Everything had been done to make it a success, including investing a significant amount of money in the sound system. The success encouraged expansion. In the second year, the basement was made into a dining area with the same care as the initial floor. The new sound system was of the same high quality as the first but had to be played as a separate system. During the first few weeks, both the lower level and the ground level of the restaurant were filled to capacity. Then the numbers began to fall. Within a few months it was obvious that something was wrong. The owner tried to think of everything he could. The quality of the food and beverages and any changes in the menu were questioned. There had been very little staff turnover, so the same people were serving as when the house was full. What was wrong? In despair and confusion, the owner called for help.

After many customer interviews, it was finally realized that the two different sound systems, playing different music, clashed with each other and created a discordant ambient background sound, causing unconscious disquiet in those present on both floors. Harmony is defined as the pleasing interaction or appropriate combination of elements in the whole. It is also defined as a pleasing combination, through constructive interference, of musical notes. The sound waves combined in a destructive manner, creating unpleasing disharmony, literally and figuratively. Interactions of sound waves, light waves, and other electromagnetic waves can positively or adversely influence the indoor environment.

Maintenance practices influence indoor environmental quality as well. When Paulette Mae Cole, who founded ABC Home, came back to work when her daughter was ten, she found that the business, which had previously thrived under her direction, was teetering. She said, "The first thing I did was try to make a difference from the inside out. We threw out all the chemical cleaners. We replaced them with natural products, and we were able to do that for less money."[8] After implementing several other sustainability initiatives as well, business turned around.

Candle Cafe and Candle 79—strictly vegan, mostly local and organic restaurants in New York—are as green as they can be, even though they rent their buildings. Candle Cafe was the first Certified Green Restaurant named by the Green Restaurant Association in New York City, and both restaurants are perennially ranked among the greenest businesses in the country. Their sustainability practices include investing in equipment, decoration, and infrastructure in line with their values, such as energy-efficient electrical and cooking equipment and eco-friendly paints and fabrics. They educate their staff about green practices and how to implement and maintain them in the workplace. They use only nontoxic, environmentally friendly cleaning supplies and sanitizers; recycle glass, plastic, metal, grease, paper, old computers and electronics, and printer cartridges; and compost their food waste. They also purchase recycled materials whenever possible. All napkins, bath tissue, ink cartridges, menu pages, and office stationery are made from recycled materials. And they invest in wind power to help offset some of the environmental impact of running the restaurants.

Whether you own or rent, build from scratch or occupy an existing facility, there are many opportunities for both manufacturing and service companies to make their facilities greener.

Total Sustainable Building Development

Paolo Soleri is a visionary architect who created the concept of *archology*, the fusion of architecture and ecology. His archologies are ecologically integrated communities or cities. They function like a single-structure, eco-industrial development that operates as an ecological closed loop. Over the last thirty years he has overseen the construction of Arcosanti[9] in the desert north of Phoenix. This city uses about 2 percent of the land that a typical sprawled city would use for the same population density as well as a fraction of the energy and material resources.

Sustainable developers are emulating and expanding on many aspects of the archology concept. One of those developers is Tom Horton, former program director at the Rodale Institute.[10] Tom was recruited by David Butterfield, a building developer seeking help in waste management and sustainable composting and gardening. Together they created Savano, a master planned community near Tucson consisting of 2,600 homes integrated into a 110-acre eco-industrial park. They experimented with every technique employed in sustainable construction, including straw bale houses, sod houses, bermed earth houses, and every experimental and proven energy—and water-conservation technology. They even had community gardens and composting.

With the integration of housing and the eco-industrial park, the municipality realized that quantifiable significant savings were possible and invested $10 million in the development. Ultimately, this project was partnered with and then sold to Sallie Mae and became its representative "green" project. Savano became the classroom for other developers who were interested in sustainability. Because of the huge scale involved there, Tom Horton and David Butterfield proved that "size matters" and that there were big payoffs on the money spent on planning.

What they learned at Savano, they integrated into their next mega sustainability project. Forty years ago, Cancun was a forgotten wasteland region on Mexico's Caribbean Yucatan coast until a computer program selected it for development as a tourist destination.

The Mexican government's computer program also selected another site for development, Loreto Bay in Baja California. The Bank of Mexico funded the infrastructure development for both projects. Unlike Cancun, however, once the infrastructure was installed, no one did the work to develop Loreto Bay. Tom and David "rediscovered" Loreto Bay and developed it based on what they learned from Savano. Chief among those lessons was full transparency to investors and the public, including communicating their vision.

The Loreto Bay project is committed to placing two-thirds of the land into permanent conservation and to being a net producer of renewable energy, water, and food/biodiversity. For the water, this means that no net amount of water is drawn from wells. Collecting rainwater and desalinating seawater produce all the water used. The development—which will consist of 5,000 homes, several hotels, and golf courses—has been a model of exquisite planning and execution. At this beautiful location, where whales mate and play, the developers got, for the first time, an exclusion from Mexico's property ownership laws so that non-Mexicans could own their beachfront homes. All the buildings are made largely from indigenous materials sourced and fabricated on-site—using a machine that rams the earth into building bricks. All the thoroughfares are free of automobiles, and there is a network of narrow roads for electric service vehicles and personal transportation. When you go food shopping, the bagger carries your bags to the electric vehicle and then drives your bags and you back home.

Tom said, "One of the coolest things we did was hire a geologist to look at the site and figure out what it looked like before Fonature, the Mexican federal tourism agency, plowed it flat. It had demolished the whole natural ecosystem. From this work we discovered where the estuaries and the channels were and we put them back. With that we reintroduced the natural water collection and filtration system. Another of the many things we did—and this was also only possible because of scale—we reused the waste heat coming off the air conditioning systems to provide all the domestic hot water."[11]

Green Building Standards

A sustainable building must consider the local environment. For centuries, buildings reflected the realities of the local climate and culture and the availability of indigenous materials. You could look at a picture of a home and tell where it was. For example, places with snow loading had homes with steep roofs. Now you cannot look at a modern building and tell where you are. You see flat roof structures in areas with high snow loads. Walls are made almost entirely out of glass in areas that are hot and have lots of sunlight. If you are looking to build a sustainable structure, tour your area and replicate the essence of whatever 100 to 200-year-old buildings you find.

For more specific guidelines, turn to sustainable design standards. In the early 1990s David had the honor of working with the fledgling U.S. Green Building Council developing a standard for sustainable buildings called Leadership in Energy and Environmental Design (LEED). The original volunteer certificants represented a tiny fraction of the entire market, but it was the beginning of a new revolution in the evolving field of green building. The certification process itself improved many buildings and inspired countless enterprises to strive to meet a higher standard. The U.S. Green Building Council[12] has created one of the most successful certification programs for structures. The new LEED v3, inaugurated in April 2009, covers commercial and residential structures for existing, new, and renovated buildings and addresses all aspects of what it entails to create a sustainable facility.

For a site itself, the LEED standard deals with reductions in the amount of construction debris, development density, and contribution to sprawl; use of a previously contaminated "brownfield" site; and access to parking, public transportation, bike storage, and the requisite changing room for those that bike, hike, or jog to work. Site development also includes maximizing open space and protecting or restoring habitats. LEED planning for the site includes quality and quantity control for storm water, light pollution, and the heat island effect—why it's cool in the woods and hot in the summer in the city.

The LEED standard addresses water use reduction for bathrooms and kitchens, as well as water use reduction for landscaping or use of gray water and on-site water treatment. In terms of energy, the LEED standard addresses the entire building's energy management system, including heating, lighting, the type of refrigerant used for cooling, energy conservation, and use of renewable energy. For materials, the standard addresses not only the types of materials used in the construction but the distance they were hauled to the site and whether they were reused or recycled materials.

In complying with the LEED standard, you'll find plenty of room to be clever and creative. Just like in the story of the tailor that killed seven flies with one swat, many criteria can be achieved with a single act. For example, the heat island effect of the roof is also mitigated when one covers the roof with photovoltaic or solar thermal panels or if one plants a rooftop garden. Implementing each of these ideas gains points toward LEED certification.

Other facility standards come from Audubon International.[13] These standards cover businesses; golf courses; schools; renovation or redevelopment; hotels, motels, inns, and bed-and-breakfasts; neighborhood or homeowner asso-ciations; new construction and development; whole villages, towns, cities, and counties; and large-scale private/destination resorts. The standard for golf courses, for example, addresses the following issues: wildlife and habitat management, chemi-cal use reduction and safety, water conservation, water quality management, and outreach and education.

For those who are extremely concerned about the impact of a building on health and human ecology, the Institute for Building Biology[14] offers courses, certification, and very rig-orous standards for building materials, indoor environments, living environments, environmental health, ecological design, building physics, and electromagnetic radiation. Accessing these standards, small to medium-sized businesses can pick and choose improvements commensurate with their budgets.

Summary

The elements of a green facility include construction materials, energy and water use and conservation, maintenance practices, and indoor environmental quality, which includes air qual-ity and electromagnetic radiation. Use building standards as a guide to green a facility. Green building standard-setting orga-nizations include the U.S. Green Building Council (Leadership in Energy and Environmental Design—LEED), Audubon International, and the Institute for Building Biology.

Here is a brief list of actions you can take:

- Source sustainable wood for every project—new or im-proved.
- Make sure the HVAC system allows plenty of fresh air.
- Fill the workspace with plants.

- Install waterless urinals.
- Let the sun do some work.
- Get rid of toxic cleaning chemicals.
- Strive for LEED certification.

Perhaps the most important aspect of a facility's environmental impact is its use of energy. The next chapter discusses renewable energy options, provides instructions for performing an energy audit, and offers recommendations for reducing energy consumption.

Energy—
Using Renewable Energy,
Energy Audits, and
Conservation

This chapter covers the basics of the sustainable use of energy, discusses the various forms of renewable energy, explains how to perform an energy audit, and provides recommendations for energy conservation.

Almost everything that moves and breathes on this planet does so because of energy it captures from the sun.[1] The energy it takes for you to move and breathe comes from the stored energy in the plant you ate or in the animal you ate, which ate a plant, which originally stored the sun's energy. When you burn a piece of wood, you are releasing the solar energy that the chloroplasts in the plant captured and that was converted to sugar and then polymerized into cellulose and lignin. When you burn fossil fuels, you are releasing solar energy that was captured by plants as long as 350 to 450 million years ago. Using oil, gas, or coal as fuel is spending the earth's capital. If you have capital and spend only the interest you earned, you can do this forever. If you spend the capital, even a tiny amount, and do this consistently over time, you will eventually run out of money. Sustainability is about using the earth's energy income and not its energy capital.

Renewable Energy

We're now at the point where renewable energy is economically viable. However, renewable energy currently supplies very little of our energy needs. About 50 percent of U.S. electricity is produced from coal, 20 percent from nuclear power, and 20 percent from natural gas. Most of the remainder is renewable hydropower.

You can power your business with renewable energy today by merely making a phone call. For a small premium, you can purchase your power from a renewable energy generator.[2] The usage portion of your bill then goes to purchase power from a renewable energy supplier, instead of your local coal-fired or nuclear power plant, thus incentivizing the development of further renewable energy resources.

You can also buy Renewable Energy Credits (RECs). RECs certify that power has been bought from renewable sources. Over 1,000 U.S. companies, educational institutions, nonprofits, and governmental institutions have bought RECs, many of them for 100 percent of the power they use, effectively powering these organizations entirely on renewable energy.[3] In twenty-three states, RECs are currently trading for $1 to $32 per 1,000 kilowatt-hours depending on the state. The pending American Clean Energy and Security Act of 2009 will create a basis for all states to employ RECs. In the not-too-distant future, a market will exist for carbon credits through the development of this "cap and trade" legislation. While one school of thought is to tax polluters, we believe that cap and trade will provide incentives for entrepreneurs to develop technology reducing the use of fossil fuels and reducing the effects of greenhouse gas emissions. Innovative opportunities exist for reducing carbon.

There are also Production Tax Credits (PTCs) for electricity from renewable sources worth $0.019 per kilowatt-hour and other incentives such as a $1-per-gallon premium paid for liquid transportation fuel made from renewable sources. Some states have net metering rules that allow renewable energy producers to sell power back to the grid at the same rate that the utility charges, effectively running the meter backward. An effective approach for reducing costs in a small to medium-sized business is to add energy-reducing technologies into all aspects of the operation.

To find the current federal, state, and utility incentives for renewable energy technologies and energy-efficiency technologies described below, check the Database of State Incentives for Renewables and Efficiency (DSIRE).[4]

HYDROPOWER

Hydropower currently meets about 6 percent of our energy needs in the United States.[5] We've pretty much tapped all the available hydropower that we can utilize without causing severe environmental consequences.

Check to see if you have a hydropower resource on your property and who owns it. If you have the right to use it, it may be the most economical power you will be able to get or is there an old water-powered building in your neighborhood that you can move into? You don't necessarily have to build a dam to use hydropower. However, unless you live in Alaska, you will have to get a Federal Energy Regulatory Commission license, regardless of how small the hydropower resource is. This license will cost you at least $200,000 and three years for permitting. One hydropower retrofit project in an old water-powered industrial building in Springfield, Massachusetts, we recently worked on has a 35-foot head (vertical drop in elevation—the greater the head, the greater the power) and a flow rate of 70 cubic feet per second. With the licensing, the total cost for the retrofit was $650,000. The project had a 165 kilowatt (kW) rated capacity and produced 700,000 kWh per year. With a $10,000 per year maintenance cost, it produced electricity at $0.11 per kWh.

WIND POWER

Wind is the fastest growing new source of power in the United States and the rest of the world. Yet wind energy merely supplies just over 1 percent of the United States' power. But it is now economically viable. According to a report by the Congressional Research Service,[6] the 2008 levelized cost of energy per megawatt-hour for wind was $67, pulverized coal was $64, nuclear power $60, and natural gas $63, placing wind largely at parity with these other sources of power. With the inevitable trends and incentives, wind looks to be the winner in the near term for cost-effective renewable energy.

The United States is committed to using wind power as the primary means to move toward energy independence and is pushing for 20 percent of U.S. power to be produced by wind in twenty years. Only Denmark is currently at this 20 percent rate. The largest wind machines (up to 5 megawatts [MW]) are producing power at a rate of about $0.09 per kWh.

Medium-sized wind machines (less than 1 MW) are ideal for farms; small wind farms; schools, colleges, and universities; government complexes; and shopping malls. They are now producing power at approximately $0.20 per kWh before RECs, PTCs, and so on. Next-generation wind technology, which puts multiple wind rotors on the same tower, promises to lower the cost of wind energy to below $0.05 per kWh and to make practical the deployment of floating wind machines moored far enough from the coast so that they are not visible from the shore.

With up to $0.07 per kWh in incentives and with electricity currently averaging $0.10 per kWh in the United States (and higher in places like New England) and only going up, wind is a smart option. If your facility is in an area where average winds are greater than 13 miles per hour and you are not using wind power, you are letting your money blow away. Aeronautica Windpower is the only company that manufacturers midsized wind turbines of 250 and 750 kW (suitable for small and medium-sized organizations) in the United States.[7]

SOLAR ENERGY

In this section we'll discuss two ways to capture the sun's energy—photovoltaics and solar thermal collectors.

Photovoltaics

Cost-effectively turning sunlight directly into electricity—that is the holy grail of renewable energy. Photovoltaic technology has been around for a long time. It consists principally of a thin slice of a semiconducting material, like monocrystalline silicon, oriented perpendicular to the sun. The sun's photons collide with the cell and kick off an electron, producing DC (direct current) power. Photovoltaics are also now made from thin films of semiconducting material.

The best photovoltaics are only about 15 percent efficient, and at $15 per square foot, they end up producing power at a cost of more than $2,500 per kW. Additional limitations: the sun does not shine at night and on cloudy days, nor does it shine the same throughout the United States. According to SolarBuzz, the price of solar electricity from photovoltaics for a home ranges from 35 to 78 cents per kWh.[8]

However, the price of photovoltaics is going down all the time. The Chinese solar cell manufacturer Suntech is selling them for close to $1,000 per kW. Check SolarBuzz periodically to see if the price of electricity from photovolatics is below what you pay.

The message here is install photovoltaics if (1) you don't have a choice (in remote locations), (2) you've got money to waste, or (3) you can get someone else to pay for all or part of it. The third case is quite common. A lot of grant funds are available for installing photovoltaics and a lot of utilities are happy to subsidize your installation.

For example, Real Goods' Solar Living Institute hosts Solar 2000, the largest photovoltaic array in northern California. The 130 kW array cost $750,000 to build and received $430,000 in California energy rebates. It produces 160,000 kWh per year.

Solar Thermal Collectors

Besides capturing solar energy with photovoltaics, you can capture the sun's energy as heat. This heat can be used for electricity generation and for space and water heating. This is called solar thermal. From 1983 to 1991, nine commercial-scale solar thermal plants were installed in the California desert. Many of these plants use mirrors to concentrate solar energy to boil a fluid, producing electricity. Totaling 354 MW in installed capacity, these plants have produced 11,000 gigawatt hours and more than $1.7 billion in revenue over the last 22 years, and they are still operational.

An area only 92 miles by 92 miles filled with solar thermal collectors would be sufficient to provide the United States and Europe with all their electrical requirements. This is an area equal to the footprint of existing U.S. coal mines.

Because solar thermal collectors, at 84 percent efficiency, are more efficient than the most efficient crystalline photovoltaics, at 15 percent efficiency, and because PV costs $15 per square foot compared to solar thermal collectors at $2, solar thermal energy is currently about forty times more cost-effective than PV. There are *no* technological, legislative, or cost barriers to solar thermal's energy competitiveness with existing, conventional energy sources right now.

Forty-five percent of the U.S. average household energy dollar goes to space heating and hot water, and the number is 63 percent in New England. It's not as sexy as photovoltaics, but solar thermal is a no-brainer. If you have rooftop space that has an unobstructed view to the south throughout the year, that is where you should invest your first renewable energy dollar. And it's so simple; you can even do this yourself. Start with a sheet of glass. Glass is invisible to visible light but opaque to infrared light (heat). Next get a sheet of aluminum and paint one side nonglossy black. Black absorbs all visible light and converts it to infrared. Put the black side facing the glass, leaving a space in between of a few inches. Build an insulated box around the layers except for the glass surface. Put this box up on your roof. Have its glass side face south, tilted at an angle equal to your latitude (Boston and Chicago, 42°; New York, 41°; Washington, DC, 39°; San Francisco, 38°; Los Angeles, 34°; Dallas, 33°; Miami, 26°).

The glass lets the sunlight in, where it is converted to infrared when it hits the black surface. Because glass does not transmit infrared, the heat is trapped in the box. Drill a hole in the bottom and the top of the box between the glass and the aluminum. If you pump cold air into the bottom, warm air will come out the top when the sun is shining. Want hot water instead of heat? Weld copper pipe to the aluminum and pump cold water through it.

A 29-square-foot flat plate solar collector in the Northeast on a mildly cloudy day takes in about 21 thousand British thermal units (MBtu) per day (22 megajoules per day).[9] The same system in San Diego would take in about 42 MBtu per day, twice the energy as in the Northeast. In Vermont, you could buy a two-panel system with a 30 percent discount from Acorn Energy Coop[10] for which you would also get a 30 percent federal tax credit and a $900 rebate from Vermont. If you were to buy your system from Co-op Power[11] in Massachusetts, which provides community-owned sustainable energy solutions throughout New England and New York, you would get a 30–40 percent discount in addition to the 30 percent federal tax credit and a 15 percent state tax credit. Co-op Power's business development manager, Lynn Benander, has had a three-panel system for ten years in her multigenerational household. Her documented savings on a system that would now cost $7,000–$10,000 before the tax credits is $1,200–$1,440 per year, which provides for a five- to seven-year payback.[12] For warmer and sunnier parts of the country, the savings get better, especially if state incentives are good. Check DSIRE for current incentives.[13]

BIOMASS/BIOFUEL

Solar energy captured by plants and used as a fuel is referred to as biomass and biofuels. In 2006 approximately 55 billion kWh of electricity was produced in the United States from biomass—20 percent of the output of all of the U.S. hydroelectric facilities. In addition, in 2004 the United States consumed 4 billion gallons of ethanol and biodiesel. U.S. law now requires that biofuel use be increased to 7.5 billion gallons by 2012, representing approximately 5 percent of gasoline's volume. In 2006, while waste-to-energy provided 0.4 percent of total U.S. energy consumption, biofuels provided 0.8 percent and biomass/wood-derived fuels 2.2 percent.

A legitimate concern about some biofuels, such as corn-based ethanol and soy-based biodiesel, is that using food as a fuel source reduces the quantity and raises the price of food. However, new technologies exist to make biofuels that don't reduce the food supply and that appear to be able to produce biofuels at less than $1 per gallon. These include technologies that (1) employ microbes to digest sawdust and excrete ethanol; (2) convert crop waste, forest trimmings, and municipal solid waste into refinable oils, and (3) utilize the energy content in waste to make natural gas and ethanol. (We'll develop these ideas further in chapter 11.)

Currently, most ethanol is made from cornstarch. Corn is a cheap cattle feed, but the cornstarch portion does not make milk or milk fat when fed to dairy cows. The protein portion can be separated in making ethanol and fed to livestock. In most places, ethanol is blended with gasoline to produce a 10 percent ethanol mix with E-10 signage at the gas pump. Most automobile manufacturers sell "flexible fuel vehicles" for no additional charge that automatically switch from 100 percent gasoline to E-10 to E-85 (85 percent ethanol fuel). If you live in the Midwest, where there is an abundance of ethanol, getting a flexible fuel vehicle the next time you buy a car is a smart move.

Biodiesel is often made from extracting the oil content from soybeans. The protein-rich soy meal is subsequently fed to livestock. Many states now require that their fleets of non-emergency vehicles that burn diesel and their buildings that are heated with heating oil use a minimum amount (e.g., 20 percent) of biodiesel. B-20 is biodiesel made from 80 percent petroleum and 20 percent of some biologically derived oil. Many municipal, state, and federal vehicles are now fueled by "yellow grease"—used fry oil that is collected from local restaurants.

How do you get your business involved in biomass/biofuel? You can buy land and plant trees to be used for fuel. With hardwood trees, you can sustainably harvest about one cord of wood per acre per year. This will produce about 18–22 million Btu, the equivalent of 3–4 barrels of oil. If the land you buy and plant is currently void of trees, you could also get carbon credits for planting these trees. Make sure you let your wood age to dry. A cord of wood that is 20 percent moisture content contains 800 pounds of water. The amount of energy it takes to evaporate all that water is the equivalent of 8 gallons of gasoline.

If your business produces any food waste, crop waste, or plant fiber/forest product waste, this material can be dried and burned to produce hot air, hot water, steam, or electricity. Some power plants in the United States up to 50 MW use wood or wood pulp as fuel sources. By using combustion methods that allow for extremely hot burn zones, catalytic converters, and other mitigation technologies, polluting emissions can be eliminated.

If you have a restaurant, commissary, food-processing operation, or catering facility with a deep fryer, your used fry oil can be used as fuel. The average fast-food restaurant disposes of about 10 gallons of fry oil per day. The energy content of this fry oil is enough to meet the average fast-food restaurant's hot water needs. Soon you will be able to get, for about $5,000 installed, an integrated fry-oil-burner hot water heater developed by Tom Leue of Yellow Biodiesel[14] that burns filtered but unprocessed used fry oil and provides a six-month to one-year payback. Waste cooking oils also can be recovered and used to help run your vehicles or process equipment. Our friend Zak Zaidman, of Kopali Organics, which makes yummy chocolates from organic, sustainably harvested ingredients from the rain forest, runs his tour bus on used fry oil picked up all around the country as his bus visits his various customers in the food business.[15] Joe was the proud driver of the bus in the annual Wellfleet, Massachusetts, Fourth of July parade, raising awareness for grease-powered transportation. He literally pumped the grease from the Dumpster at a fried food restaurant and drove to Virginia on the fuel.

If your organic waste is wet, it can generally be dewatered and then burned. If it cannot be dewatered, wet organic material can be placed in an anaerobic digester. This is merely an enclosed body of water (tank or covered lagoon) where oxygen is kept from the liquid. Anaerobic organisms break down the digestible organic solids, releasing methane gas. The gas can be used to run a burner, boiler, or generator.

Stonyfield Farm used to feed yogurt waste, resulting from its extensive quality control (QC) sampling, to pigs. Stonyfield CEO Gary Hirshberg said, "Now we will have a screw press that separates the yogurt from the cup, and the yogurt will go to an anaerobic digester and become methane."[16] Anaerobic digesters can be "home grown" and scaled down to accommodate a single residence or scaled up to handle the sewage of an entire city.

GEOTHERMAL ENERGY

At Breitenbush Spa in Oregon, seventy fissures in the earth bring water up to the surface at temperatures between 180°F and 270°F. All the buildings at this site are heated with geothermal power. Capers Food headquarters in Vancouver, British Columbia, was also powered by a geothermal resource. In Iceland, 26 percent of electricity and 86 percent of heating comes from geothermal power. If you live near the Pacific Rim of Fire, near any volcanoes or any hot springs, you may have a geothermal resource near you.[17]

Even in places where the geothermal heat resource is poor, at 4 feet down the temperature of the earth is constantly 50°F.

Instead of heating from subzero up to 70°F in the winter and cooling down from more than 80°F in the summer, you can tap into this 50°F geothermal resource, using implanted subterranean coils or heat exchangers and heat pumps, and lower your use of fossil fuel and other nonrenewables in heating and cooling. Costs have largely to do with the nature of your subterranean strata (getting through solid rock is expensive). This type of geothermal power can be installed by many HVAC contractors such as Bourke Builders,[18] which was the first certified geothermal system installer in New England.

Because a geothermal system takes heat and dumps it into the ground (which is 50°F) for air conditioning, geothermal power is essentially free, using almost no energy to produce air conditioning. For heating, instead of heating up from outside ambient temperatures that could be below freezing, it only needs to heat up from the 50°F temperature of the ground, so a geothermal system uses about one-quarter the electricity of an electric heating system. It also makes hot water with one-quarter the electricity of electric water heating. The capital costs of a system for a building of 2,000 to 5,000 square feet are about $20,000–$25,000, with $7,000–$14,000 of that the cost for the underground heat exchanger loop. If you are installing this system in a new facility, the entirety of the system costs, including ducting, controls, and so on, qualifies for the 30 percent federal tax credit.

The Energy Audit

The cheapest kilowatt-hour of electricity or gallon of fuel you will find is the one you don't use. Besides producing your own energy, the path to sustainability requires that you conserve energy—waste less and use what you do use more efficiently.

In a typical business, energy is used for heating, air conditioning, hot water, lighting, refrigeration, transportation (including freight in and out), commuting, operation of office and manufacturing equipment, facilities maintenance, and sending and receiving of mail and packages.

"If you can measure it, you can manage it" is true for energy, too. In order to conserve energy, you must first make a baseline of what your current use is by conducting an energy audit.

To perform your energy audit, first collect your monthly energy bills for the previous year. Depending on how you buy energy, you may have separate meters for lighting, air conditioning, machines, and so on, or you may have a single bill. The more granularity you have, the better picture of your energy use you can make.

The types of energy you use come in different units. Transportation fuel and heating oil are sold in gallons, natural gas in therms or 100 standard cubic feet (scf), propane in pounds, wood in cords or tons, coal in tons, and electricity in kilowatt-hours. See resource F, the energy source calculator, to convert all these units to one standard.

You won't be able to directly calculate some of your energy use because sometimes you pay for services that use energy. These include travel, commuting, freight, postage, and expedited courier. For freight, you may pay to ship by boat, rail, truck, or air, but you don't readily know how much energy you consumed. The same is true of postage and expedited courier. Here is how to estimate your energy use in each of these areas.

CALCULATING COMMUTING ENERGY USE

To calculate energy use for commuting, first figure out how many employees work for you. What percent commute by car? What is the average distance that your average employee commutes to work? (You have gathered this information as part of the employee questionnaire in chapter 2.)

Multiply the number of employees that work for you by the percent that drive to work times the average distance that the average employee lives away from your facility times 2 (round trip) times 3,512 Btu per passenger mile.[19] Motorcycles are about twice as efficient at 1,855 Btu per mile; trains, about 3,000 Btu per mile; buses, 4,235 Btu per mile. Vanpools are the winner at 1,322 Btu per passenger mile.

CALCULATING TRAVEL ENERGY USE

You could go through your employees' expense reports to reconstruct the figure for energy use due to travel, but you can also make a very good estimate. How many employees travel on company business on the average day? What is the average distance they travel? Multiply the number of employees that travel on company business per day by the average distance they travel times 250 days per year (increase this number if you are open 6 or 7 days per week) times 3,512 Btu per mile.[20]

For air travel, do the same calculation as above. On average, where do your people fly? How many miles away is that? How many flights do your employees take per week? Multiply the average distance flown by 2 times the number of employees who fly per week times 50 (weeks per year—with vacation) times 3,261 Btu per passenger mile.[21]

CALCULATING FREIGHT ENERGY USE

To calculate your energy use for freight, you may be able to do a forensic reconstruction of your shipping records, but the following method provides a good estimate. How many pounds of product do you ship out the door each year? What is the average distance you ship your product? Do you ship internationally, nationally, mostly within the state, city, or neighborhood?

How many miles is that? How do you ship? By railroad, boat, truck, or air?

Divide the weight in pounds you ship per year by 2,000 pounds to get tons. Multiply the tons by the average distance you ship your product. Multiply that by 341 Btu per ton-mile if by rail, 510 Btu per ton-mile if by boat, 3,357 Btu per ton-mile if by truck, and 9,600 Btu per ton-mile if by air. If you ship by truck to a port from which the product is then shipped by boat, you can break down the calculation for each transportation mode. If you own your own trucks, you should be able to calculate this figure by fuel use. If you can't calculate it by fuel use and need to use this method, consider if the truck is sent out full and returns empty and then multiply the distance to the average customer by 2.

CALCULATING POSTAGE / EXPEDITED COURIER ENERGY USE

How much money did you spend on postage last year? How much on expedited couriers (UPS, FedEx, etc.)? What is the average distance to your customer or the person you are mailing to? As of this writing, postage is $0.44 per ounce. Divide the amount you spent on postage by the current postal rate for one ounce and divide that by 16 to get pounds, and then divide that by 2,000 to get tons. Multiply the tons by the average distance you sent your mail. How many ton-miles of posted material is that? Multiply this number by 3,357 Btu per ton-mile to get your postal energy usage.

For other ground shipping, use the same U.S. Postal Service factor of $0.44 per ounce and 3,357 Btu per ton-mile, even though actual ground transportation rates will be cheaper, thereby slightly underestimating your energy use. The price for air freight across the whole country is also pretty close to the postage letter rate, so use $0.44 per ounce but 9,600 Btu per ton-mile for that calculation.

CALCULATING OFFICE EQUIPMENT AND PROCESS EQUIPMENT ENERGY USE

Unless you have separate metering, equipment use is difficult to measure, but it's not so difficult to estimate.

Do you have an inventory of every item in your facility? (It's probably a good thing to have for insurance, depreciation, and other business reasons.) Every item you buy that uses electricity has a label on it that either tells you how much energy it uses in a year or has a rating like X watts, Y volts, or Z amps. Volts times amps equals watts, so make an inventory of the office and process equipment you use, what each item's watt rating is, and the number of hours of use per year. This will give you a kilowatt-hour figure per item-year.

Now you should have a complete picture of your total energy use. In addition to preparing a table showing Btu use per category, also calculate the percent of the total energy use in each category. This will allow you to focus your energy conservation efforts in the areas where you have the greatest impact. Once you have this information, communicate it to your employees.

Energy Conservation Recommendations

Obviously, recommendations specific to your situation would require review of the results of your own energy audit. Below are some general recommendations for energy conservation.

HEATING / HOT WATER

Make sure your facility is properly insulated and sealed against infiltration. Many energy providers will perform an energy assessment of your facility as part of their demand-side management programs. This service may also come from other sources. The assessor may take infrared pictures of your facility to show where heat is escaping. He or she also may use a blower to overpressure your facility to try to find where air is leaking out (or in). Make sure that your facility takes in fresh air.

The correct amount of fresh air intake for most businesses is 20 cubic feet per minute per employee. This means that 20 cubic feet per minute is also leaving the facility. To ensure that the air that is leaving is not taking your heat or air conditioning with it, consider installing countercurrent air-to-air heat exchangers. These devices work on the same principle that allows whales to swim in arctic waters without losing body heat through their fins. The warm inside air is used to warm the incoming cold air on its way in, so that by the time the fresh air enters the room, it is heated to the room's temperature by the exiting air. By the time it leaves the building, the exiting air is the same temperature as the outside air.

In areas with high ceilings, make sure that you install ceiling fans or other ways of pushing the hot air back down to the workers during the heating season. During the cooling season, turn those fans off. Cold air falls, and there is no energy win in pulling down ceiling air that is hotter because of its proximity to the roof (which is frequently a blacktop solar absorber).

Check the thickness of your insulation or its R value to see if it is sufficient for your climate. If you can't see the insulation, you can measure the room air temperature, outside air temperature, and the temperature of the inside surface of the outside walls. The closer the wall temperature is to the inside air temperature, the better insulated your facility is. See what the temperature difference is for those areas where you know what level of insulation you have and compare it to those areas where you don't know to determine where the most insulation is needed.

See if your hot water heaters and storage tanks could benefit from extra insulation, as well as the pipes between the heater and the storage tanks and between the storage tanks and the rest of the facility. If you're installing new hot water capacity, consider installing tankless on-demand water heaters. They are available for both electricity and gas.

For hot water, Laury Hammel's Longfellow Clubs uses multiple solutions. To conserve energy and provide for all the needs of their 10,000 members, they use a variety of technologies, including solar hot water and cogeneration. Laury recalls, "At our Natick club, we have a cogeneration unit. We burn natural gas and create electricity, and the waste heat from the electricity is heating all of the pools and some of the showers. It is saving us so much energy. We are close to 100 percent efficient because whatever energy is not used to make electricity is used to make heat.

"As far as we know, we have the largest solar hot water system in the Northeast. The solar hot water system has a 3.5-year payback. We got a check for $35,000 from the utility for this $145,000 system 1.5 months after we installed it. We borrowed money from the members to finance the solar hot water system. The cogeneration system was paid for by the company that installed it, and we split all the savings, with us getting 10 percent and them 90 percent. We save $12,000 per year. After ten years we get to buy the equipment."[22]

When installing heating equipment, try to get the most efficient equipment you can. Typical gas furnaces from the 1970s have an annual fuel utilization efficiency (AFUE) of about 65 percent. EPA requires a new furnace to have an efficiency of at least 78 percent. Multistage modulating gas furnaces can provide 92–97 percent efficiencies, so there is a big range in furnace performance. Remember that the ductwork is an integral part of the heating systems. The U.S. Department of Energy (DOE) states that about 20 percent of heat energy ends up leaking through the ductwork.[23] Check to see whether a heat pump would benefit your facility.

DOE and EPA jointly created a program over a decade ago called Energy Star[24] for rating energy efficiency in a variety of items, such as furnaces and appliances. It is a single parameter rating and the bar is not that high—most manufacturers can get an Energy Star, and in the heating category, Energy Star ratings start at only 15 percent above the new product standard. But the ratings will give you some guidance about heating, air conditioning, lighting, office equipment, and programmable controls.

Programmable controls are really the key to maximizing energy conservation. When not occupied, spaces should be minimally heated to prevent pipes from bursting when the weather is cold and not air conditioned when the weather is hot. Automated controls are one of the most inexpensive solutions to energy conservation. In large buildings, the right type of controls has been shown to cut heating bills in half.

At the Longfellow Clubs, Laury said, "We are in the process right now of developing an energy management system—it enables us to use economizers in the heating system. It will be an integrated, completely automated system to manage the heat so that the heat is going on at the right time and turned off at the right time—much easier to monitor and user friendly. The whole idea is to give people the ability to make changes but not be reliant on the staff to manage the heating. We will be buying new air conditioners and heat pumps that we are paying for out of the savings in the energy, and we will own these. We are being loaned money based on our prospective savings."[25]

Use every opportunity to recover waste heat to use for process heating or even cogeneration. This can be done with water-to-water, water-to-air, air-to-water, and air-to-air heat exchangers (described above). At Loreto Bay, Tom Horton employed heat exchangers to capture the waste heat from the air conditioners to use for heating water.

Consider, too, using the waste heat of your neighbors' operations.

AIR CONDITIONING/REFRIGERATION

The Environmental Research Laboratory in Tucson has developed some remarkable technology (for Disney, Biosphere 2, and others), including a solar-powered air conditioning system.[26] One of these systems is at its facility at the Tucson airport and another at Real Goods' Solar Living Center in Hopland, California. The one in California has lavender plants growing on it, so you can stand in the center's parking lot when it is 100°F out and be blasted with cold air laced with lavender scent. If you are in an area that is both hot and dry, this may be a perfect cooling system for you.

If you aren't in such an area, consider open cycle cooling systems like cooling towers as opposed to closed Rankine cycle type cooling systems, which use a refrigerant (like propane, ammonia, or a fluorocarbon).

Consider installing air conditioning equipment with an adaptive, variable motor controller that adjusts fan speed and electricity use based on the needs of the compressor. You can enjoy energy savings of 20–60 percent, with an average of 35 percent. Adaptive, variable motor controllers are also excellent to use on manufacturing equipment that has a variable load.

Fuel-burning electricity-generating equipment is only about 33 percent efficient. This means that two-thirds of the energy in the fuel burned at such a plant is lost in the cooling towers or smokestacks. Once it leaves the generator, another 7.2 percent is lost in transmission and distribution, leaving a net of 30 percent of the energy in the original fuel delivered as electricity.

It takes 144 Btu of energy to melt 1 pound of ice at 32°F to water at 32°F. When it melts, 1 ton of ice produces 288,000 Btu of cooling. That's the equivalent cooling power of about 8 gallons of oil used to make electricity. You need about 1.3 cubic yards to store 1 ton of ice. If your facility is in a place that is frozen much of the winter and you have the space, consider building a facility to make and store ice in the winter to use for refrigeration and cooling.

Refrigerated warehouses and trucks take less energy to maintain their cool or cold temperatures when they are full (wall to wall and floor to ceiling). Also, make sure you install strip doors or curtains and dock seals to prevent energy loss when workers move between temperature-controlled and ambient-temperature areas or use insulated bulkheads in your reefer trucks when they are carrying a reduced load.

LIGHTING

Effective January 2014, the manufacture and sale of incandescent bulbs of greater than 40 watts and less than 150 watts will be banned in the United States. In Canada and Europe they will be banned in 2012. Good riddance. Only 1 percent of the energy that goes into an incandescent bulb is converted into light. Incandescent lights are basically heaters that have a byproduct of a small amount of light. A 100-watt incandescent light gives off about 17 lumens per watt. (A lumen is a measure of visible light.)

A 7-watt bulb emits only 6 lumens per watt. Incandescent bulbs' direct replacements, CFLs, emit 40–70 lumens per watt. Their older siblings, linear fluorescent lights, emit 30–110 lumens per watt.

At 140 lumens per watt, a 1,000-watt high-pressure so-dium lamp has a 24,000-hour life with a bulb cost of $40–$100. At $0.15 per kWh, if it is turned on all the time, this bulb would save $1,315 per year in electricity costs over the equivalent wattage of the best CFLs. Don't know where you'd put a 1,000-watt lamp (equivalent to a 2,000-watt CFL)? In the basement or attic, of course—with fiber optic cables coming from it to deliver light all over your facility. The telecommunications industry has made fiber optics so cheap that it now pays to fiber optically wire your facility to a central or local lighting system. This same system can deliver daylight during the daytime too.

White light emitting diodes (LEDs) have made a lot of progress at being cost-effective lighting choices. They provide light at 10–150 lumens per watt, which is in the range of other light sources. However, because they put out light in a single direction, they are more efficient for many applications.

Don't like the way things look in fluorescent light? You can fix that easily by selecting lights with different phosphors. The way fluorescents work is that they have a bit of mercury vapor inside that marginally conducts a current, exciting the electrons in the mercury atom's orbits and causing them to emit ultraviolet light. The ultraviolet light then fluoresces a phosphor coated on the inside of a glass tube. Actually, it is not a phosphor but three phosphors—one to make red, one to make blue, and one to make green. When combined, they produce white light. These phosphors are pretty much the same ones you would find coating the screen of a color television tube. Many, many phosphors are available that influence the color and quality of the light produced. Most CFLs and fluorescents have phosphors that do a better job of simulating sunlight than incandescents do. You can also buy full-spectrum fluorescent lights that reproduce natural lighting well enough that you can grow plants indoors with them. They also sterilize the air like natural sunlight. There is no wrong or right color. The choice is completely subjective.

Lighting has a profound influence on point-of-purchase product appeal, so even if most of your facility uses one type of lighting, take the time to go to a lighting center with some of the products you might display to see how they look under various types of energy-efficient lighting.

Sodium vapor lights and fluorescents all have mercury in them. However, current CFLs are manufactured with one-tenth or less of the mercury they used to have, and the amount of mercury emitted into the atmosphere from coal-burning power plants is much more per lumen output for incandescents than for fluorescents and sodium vapor lights.

You can also save energy by putting in occupancy sensors where you can get away with it. However, they are not much good in offices where people are sedentary. It is demoralizing for people to have to intentionally move every 5 to 10 minutes to prevent the lights from going out. In such cases, the best thing to do is create a culture at work that makes it socially unacceptable to leave the light on if you're the last person to leave the room. However, conference rooms, hotel rooms, manufacturing facilities that use robots, and storage rooms can all benefit from occupancy sensors, and they are not that expensive.

TRAVEL

Try to get as many ultraefficient vehicles, flexible fuel vehicles, and diesels running on biofuels in your fleet as possible. Look into the new German Loremo (150 miles per gallon [mpg]) and the Gem electric car for travel near your facility, especially if you will be putting your name or logo on the side of these cars. They are novel enough looking that you will get extra marketing mileage out of their use.

Joe rides a bike 13 miles to the office and 13 miles home, in all four seasons, and David drives hybrid electric vehicles. Don't assume a car is efficient just because it is a hybrid. Many of the hybrids on the market use the hybrid technology as a performance enhancement and not to save energy. If a hybrid gets less than 40 mpg, the technology is just a performance enhancement. You can get more than 40 mpg on some conventional cars.

It is important to travel to meet with existing or prospective customers, clients, suppliers, colleagues, and others. With webinars, Skype, instant messaging, e-mailable PowerPoint presentations and videoconferencing, podcasts, and other technologies, you can get away with traveling less, but don't sabotage your business by eliminating travel to enhance your sustainability. Out-of-business companies are not sustainable. Remember, combining "high-tech with high-touch" demonstrates the full spectrum of sustainable possibilities, including the "human touch."

FREIGHT AND POSTAGE

You should always judge your direct-mail marketing pieces with an eye for their cost-effectiveness. Mal Warwick, who runs a direct-mail marketing company primarily serving nonprofits, says, "We analyze our clients' mailing lists and typically cut down a mailing list by 60–70 percent. It's just not cost-effective for our clients to mail to so many addresses. We also encourage them to eliminate front-end premiums, like free address labels. They guilt a person into first-time giving, but there is generally no membership renewal and, in the end, it costs more to acquire these types of members than they donate."[27]

One of the best steps you can take to reduce your freight impact is to ship electronically. Many companies provide music, books, and software as downloads rather than sending a disc. Joe tells his friends, "Don't buy this book!" After they uncross their eyes, he tells them to buy and download the electronic version instead. For hard goods, use a boat or rail when you can, truck (ground) if you can't use boat or rail, and air only when absolutely necessary.

Modify your order picking, packing, and shipping so that you don't send multiple packages to the same customer from the same facility on the same day that you could ship in a single package. Similarly, modify your back-order system so that if multiple items are back-ordered, you pick, pack, and ship at the end of the day. Or at least wait until after the last incoming packages have been received and sorted. Motherwear saved a fortune and much environmental waste by preventing multiple boxes from being shipped to the same person the same day by adopting these measures. Consider drop shipping whenever you can.

For all of these recommendations, include action steps in your employees' measures of performance, empowering them to take charge of an action and to make a difference. You'll find more about this in chapter 1.

Summary

A variety of creative and innovative alternative energy systems are available for the sustainable business. Basically, all alternatives attempt to avoid using fossil fuels and nonrenewable energy. The simplest step is purchasing renewable energy from your energy supplier. Capturing energy from nature provides the next best step: hydropower, wind power, solar power, biomass/biofuel, and geothermal power.

As we mentioned in chapter 2, it will be useful to conduct an energy audit to determine your energy strengths and weaknesses and to uncover opportunities for energy savings. During the audit, you will measure commuting, travel, freight, postage and outside couriers, office equipment, HVAC, hot water, lighting, and production techniques.

Here are some of the steps you can follow:

- Contact your energy supplier and determine if you can purchase renewable energy or renewable energy credits.
- Research alternative energy possibilities for your neighborhood, climate, and facility.
- Conduct an energy audit.
- Carpool, travel less, turn off the lights, and insulate.
- Use your waste for energy.
- Reduce, reuse, and recycle energy.
- Reduce using and moving paper by using electronic communications and downloading documents and books.

Reducing energy use has a direct impact on one's carbon footprint. The next chapter provides guidance on calculating your enterprise's carbon footprint.

Carbon— Quantifying and Reducing Your Carbon Footprint

In the near future, enterprises of all sizes will need to consider and address their carbon footprints—the amount of carbon dioxide that they produce. This chapter provides a short explanation of the greenhouse warming effect and indicates how upcoming regulations are likely to affect corporations. Then you'll learn how to determine what your carbon footprint is and how to reduce it cost-effectively.

The Greenhouse Warming Effect

The glass roof of a greenhouse allows visible light to travel through, where it is absorbed and becomes heat (infrared), but the glass does not transmit infrared heat, so the heat stays trapped in the greenhouse. Carbon dioxide and certain other gases in the earth's atmosphere have a similar effect. They trap heat near the earth's surface.

The gases that have been officially identified by the UN under the Kyoto Protocol as greenhouse gases are carbon dioxide, methane, and nitrous oxide, and certain fluorinated gases (CFCs) like Freon. Each molecule of methane traps 23 times as much heat as each molecule of carbon dioxide. Nitrous oxide traps 296 times as much. For CFCs, the numbers are even higher.

While the United States is not a signatory to the Kyoto Protocol and does not yet regulate carbon emissions, the Securities and Exchange Commission (SEC) now requires public companies to disclose their greenhouse gas emissions. In the future, if you run a small to medium-sized company interested in doing business with a government agency, you may be required to disclose your climate risks through your operations. Minimizing your carbon footprint will become a competitive advantage. The trend indicates that regulation for all polluting emissions and releases is inevitable. Businesses will no longer be able to externalize costs and use the environment as a private profit center and dumping ground.

An August 2009 study of half of the S&P 500 companies found that, for example, chemical companies produce carbon emissions averaging 868 metric tons of CO_2 per million dollars in revenue. Based on the projection of $15 per metric ton of CO_2 in 2011 under the proposed cap and trade program and $26 per metric ton in 2019, chemical companies could have carbon costs of 5.5 percent of earnings in 2011 and 9.6 percent of earnings in 2019, with the range going up to 25 percent of EBITDA (earnings before interest, taxes, depreciation, and amortization) in 2019.[1]

What You Can Do

One of this book's themes is "if you can measure it, you can manage it." So the first step in reducing your carbon footprint is to measure how much carbon dioxide you are currently producing. Every action your company takes, every bit of energy you expend, results in a corresponding emission or sequestration of carbon dioxide. Collectively, these emissions add up to your organization's carbon footprint.

Measuring is how it all starts. Gary Hirshberg, CEO of Stonyfield Farm, is also board chair of Climate Counts.[2] Climate Counts uses a 0-to-100-point scale and twenty-two criteria to determine if companies have

- Measured their climate footprint
- Reduced their impact on global warming
- Supported progressive climate legislation
- Publicly disclosed their climate actions clearly and comprehensively

Several organizations,[3] such as Carbon Concierge,[4] use online tools for calculating your carbon footprint, or you can use the simple method explained in this chapter and resource G. Whichever method you choose, start calculating your carbon baseline by knowing your energy use. Chapter 7 and resource F contain information on how to measure and inventory energy use, expressed in terms of a fuel or energy source and how many million Btu you used. You can take those numbers and put them in column A of the carbon footprint calculator in resource G to calculate your carbon footprint.

Once you know your carbon footprint, you can balance it by paying "penance." Your organization can buy carbon credits from organizations such as SocialCarbon,[5] RainTrust Foundation,[6] Cantor Fitzgerald,[7] Element Markets,[8] Evolution Markets,[9] and others. Let's be very clear about this: while almost every environmental solution listed in this book also has a bottom-line benefit to an organization, buying carbon offsets seems like it is just a cost without a direct benefit to the company.

A more thoughtful and rewarding approach could be to look more carefully at how you operate and consider making changes to actually reduce your carbon footprint (before paying penance for whatever you are unable to mitigate). For example, when Laury Hammel installed a cogeneration system at one of his Longfellow health clubs, he not only saved money but also saved 310 tons of carbon dioxide per year.

Some of the best ways to mitigate your carbon footprint are to plant trees in places where none exist, mine methane gas from landfills (and either flare it or use it to generate power), and dry and burn animal waste or decompose it in a way in which the methane it emits is captured and flared or used to generate power.

Consider other activities you engage in that produce carbon dioxide or other greenhouse warming gases. For example, the U.S. EPA Climate Leaders program notes that the 2 billion livestock in the United States significantly contribute to methane emissions. Does your business involve fermentation, animal husbandry, or manure management? If you have a dairy or hog farm, do you have any anaerobic lagoons or holding tanks? Do you own or operate a landfill or do you compost on your property? (Unless you are using an in-vessel static aerated composting system, most of the material you are composting is undergoing some sort of anaerobic decomposition. This results in the production of ammonia, volatile organic compounds, and methane in addition to carbon dioxide, which in this case is "carbon neutral.")

For every ton wet weight of manure, wet organics, or similar material you have in an anaerobic lagoon, compost pile, or landfill, you may be producing methane at the equivalent global warming capacity of about ¼ ton of carbon dioxide.[10] The methane can be captured, producing renewable energy and eliminating its carbon footprint, even with the inefficiency of most methane recapture efforts. If you own a landfill and are tapping the methane gas, you are probably losing to the environment four times as much methane as you are capturing.

Do you run a sewage or wastewater treatment plant? The methane you outgas should be captured and either flared or used to power something. Multiply the amount of methane gas you emit (in tons) into the atmosphere by 23. This is the equivalent CO_2 greenhouse warming effect of the methane. Do you use nitrous oxide as an anesthesia or as a propellant in aerosol cans? Multiply the amount of nitrous oxide you emit (in tons) by 296. This is the equivalent CO_2 greenhouse warming effect of the nitrous oxide.

Many other non-energy-related sources produce greenhouse warming gases. Once you know the total CO_2 equivalent that you produce, subtract the amount of carbon sequestration you are responsible for. For example, if you are growing crops and you switch from annual tilling to no-till agriculture, you are causing an average of 0.223 ton of carbon (0.816 ton of CO_2) to be sequestered per acre not tilled annually.[11]

Carbon credits are being awarded for putting manure into a lined hole and flaring the methane gas that is emitted with, for example, up to 5 tons of carbon credits per cow-year.

Trees take in carbon dioxide, producing wood and oxygen, and can effectively store and sequester CO_2. If you allow them to grow for many decades, they become a carbon sink. Trees like loblolly pines, ponderosa pines, and black walnuts sequester between 5.5 and 17 tons of CO_2 per year after the first ten years.[12]

An existing tree does not accrue carbon gas credits. It is and has been already sequestering carbon dioxide and is part of the global CO_2 balance equation. What you get credits for—what truly mitigates atmospheric carbon dioxide—is if you change empty land into forestland by planting trees. Then you are increasing the amount of carbon that is sequestered, decreasing the amount of global carbon dioxide. Even if the land is currently in cultivation, the crop will be harvested and decompose, giving up within a short period of time (perhaps less than one year) the CO_2 that it sequestered during its growing cycle.

Almost twenty years ago, and well before the UN's Kyoto Protocol was put into effect, Joe took a chemically contaminated urban site in Springfield, Massachusetts (the current location of CSRwire.com, Meadowbrook Lane Capital, the Gasoline Alley Foundation, and Social(k), among others), that was barren of life and planted hundreds of plants, trees, grasses, flowers, and cactus. Not only did they bioremediate the chemical contaminants but they also sequestered carbon dioxide.

Land that has been clear-cut and is not being replanted, urban land, and farmland that are converted to forestry are all candidates for carbon credits because they genuinely increased the amount of sequestered carbon dioxide. If a natural disaster (for example, a volcanic eruption, an avalanche, a flood, or a fire) strips an area of its trees, you can serve the planet and earn carbon credits to offset your carbon load by planting trees and leaving them to grow for a long period of time.

This is an activity you can do without a middleman. Simply buy land and plant trees. It you want to actually get tradable credits, however, you have to register your protocol with organizations like the Chicago Climate Exchange.[13] If you plant black walnut trees, not only will you be sequestering carbon, but you will also be making your descendants rich. Black walnuts' growth rate is about 39,000 board feet per acre per year (after the first five years). Black walnut logs sell at up to $8 per board foot (not to mention the nuts you can harvest and the dyes that some craftspeople make from walnut shells).

Mitigating Global Warming on a Grand Scale

In addition to the above approaches, some novel, large-scale schemes are being proposed and debated for carbon credits. Some certified greenhouse gas mitigation projects are silly because they neither genuinely reduce greenhouse gases nor reduce the earth's temperature. Some of the proposed mitigation methodologies don't actually sequester or neutralize greenhouse gases, but rather they reduce the solar energy the earth would receive, causing the earth to cool and thereby effectively offsetting the effects of carbon dioxide. One of these schemes involves putting mirrors into space to reflect away solar energy. A more cost-effective method is to inject sulfate into the stratosphere.[14] Scientists know this method works because when volcanoes spew sulfate into the air, it has the effect of cooling. One way to do it is for giant earth-based canons to fire the sulfate up into the stratosphere. The sulfate could come from smokestack scrubbers from coal-burning power plants.

However, more down-to-earth possibilities exist. A group of respected scientists from Lawrence Livermore National Laboratory led by Hashem Akbari, an Iranian-born nuclear engineer, published a study in *Climatic Change*[15]—a peer-reviewed scientific journal—showing that the global warming effect from the CO_2 emissions of the world's 600 million cars could be offset by painting all the roofs and roads in the tropical and semitropical regions white, thus reflecting sunlight back into space. The value of this in terms of carbon credits would be $1 trillion—more than the cost to buy and apply the white paint.

Small businesses can find large and small opportunities to be creative in mitigating CO_2. If you grow wood on existing forestland, harvest it, replant the trees with new trees, and store the wood in a way that ensures that it would not be burned or decomposed (for example, by building a giant wooden pyramid in the desert), you should qualify for certified carbon credits. If all the empty deep shaft coal and other mines were filled with sawdust, logs, char, and crop and forest waste and sealed (kept dry), that would have a huge impact on reducing CO_2 (and perhaps provide for bequeathing coal to our descendants 250 million years from now).

Summary

Global warming is real and will soon be regulated. Be proactive about your carbon emissions:

- Use the data from your energy audit and the carbon footprint calculator to determine your carbon footprint.
- Consider whether you want to reduce your carbon footprint by buying carbon credits.
- Mitigate the production of greenhouse gases by using renewable energy.
- Sequester carbon.
- Convert methane gas and nitrous oxide into other forms.

With preceding chapters dealing with all the measures needed to create a baseline of your current environmental status, the rest of the book deals with proactive engagement. The biggest impact your enterprise may have is not in what you do but what you buy. The next chapter deals with sustainable purchasing.

Purchasing— Using Your Dollar to Save the Planet

The greatest impact companies can have is often not what they do, but what they buy and where they buy it. This chapter deals with what to buy, where to buy, who to buy from, and how to buy to ensure sustainability.

The most important message in this chapter is that you have enormous power to do good by choosing how you spend your money, whom you spend it with, and what you spend it on. And if you believe that you are too small to make a difference or to be able to influence your vendors' environmental practices, you are just plain wrong. The eight rules for sustainability purchasing will show you how.

Rule 1—You Are Responsible

First of all, let's get very clear about responsibilities and boundary conditions. Just because you are not producing the raw material or components you use does not take you off the hook of responsibility. If you buy something and use it or resell it, you own the responsibility. For example, over 90 percent of dairy product companies' environmental impact is on the farm, or, put another way, 90 percent of their impact is from the milk they buy, not from their own product production activities.

Many companies intentionally structure their enterprises to outsource the production of milk. Many believe milk, as a commodity raw material, is outside their sphere of influence. Other companies, like Ben & Jerry's and Stonyfield Farm, believe that they have a responsibility for their supply chain (what they buy and how it is produced). They reach out to their suppliers and demand milk exclusively from family farms versus factory farms and milk that is free of rBGH. Stonyfield has taken a further step and insists on certified organic milk. Both companies made a conscious decision to include standards aligned with their values in their supply chain. Gary Hirshberg, Stonyfield CEO, said, "Our biggest environmental issue/impact is milk. Historically, we have always provided incentives to the farmers to do the stuff we wanted them to do. And when times get hard, we also help them survive."[1]

Don't simply adopt the specifications vendors offer you. Take the ethical high ground. When in doubt about the stability of your ethical high ground, carry your self-inquiry to an extreme. For example, would you switch suppliers if your supplier used concentration-camp labor to produce your products and, after filling your order, had the workers shoot and bury each other? What unethical business practice could you substitute for the above and still be sanguine about continuing to do business with that supplier? Your suppliers are acting on your behalf. They are representing you in the world. When you pay them for a good or service, you are giving approval to them and their methods. More than receiving approval, they are acting on your behalf. They are you.

Rule 2—The Customer Is King or Queen

Every supplier knows that the customer is king or queen. The world is large, and many, many competing suppliers would love to have your business and would do just about anything to get it. So exercise the power of your purse and buy products that help your company achieve its sustainability goals. Don't give up if your normal suppliers say they can't supply something. If a supplier keeps saying no to you, perhaps you are truly involved with someone whose business scale is so much larger than yours that you become the proverbial flea on an elephant's back, with no influence. Maybe you should switch to a supplier that feels your bite, who needs you more.

Rule 3—Ask Your Suppliers for Green Products and Services

Almost every major and minor product and service innovation comes from small and medium-sized companies, not the big companies. These innovations percolate up to the larger companies. A supplier that tunes into its innovative customers, sees the shape of the future through their eyes, and provides green products or services to them is a supplier that has a competitive advantage. When you *specify more sustainable products and services*, you are doing free market and product research and development and forecasting for your suppliers' businesses. The suppliers who understand this will thank you. The suppliers who don't are stupid, and you are not safe doing business with them.

Rule 4—Write Your Green Purchasing Specifications on Your Purchase Order Form and Prominently Display Them on Your Web Site and All Correspondence

It is so easy to use a computer or word processor to string words together. It is amazing how authoritative the words become when they are written.

Putting your values on your vision statement is nice, but if you want real results, put them on your purchase order form and on your Web site or other company literature that your vendors are sure to see. If you write your base specifications on the purchase order and on the bottom you write, "This Purchase Order Is Subject to the Terms and Conditions on the Reverse Side," and then state your sustainable terms and conditions (preferably within a text box) on the back side, your suppliers will correctly assume that you mean it. They will be concerned of possible short-term and long-term consequences if they do not comply with the contractual terms and conditions under which they agreed to accept your money.

On the other hand, if you sheepishly ask them if they can supply you with 100 percent postconsumer waste recycled content paper, they will say, "Sorry, I can't," because no is the easiest thing to say.

Rule 5—Empower Your Purchasing Agents

Make sure that your purchasing agents have bought into the program. Come up with several mutually agreed upon sustainable purchasing measures of performance, which are part of the basis for job retention, promotion, and bonuses. And make sure that you give them enough wiggle room to bend the criteria a bit on individual items as long as they meet collective goals.

Gary Hirshberg said, "Stonyfield implemented a Mission Action Program in ten areas. In purchasing, we have created green guidelines and we are getting fabulous results. What's really cool to me is that almost everyone on the purchasing team is new within the last four years. They don't just purchase with dollars; they purchase with these criteria. The head of purchasing is someone we stole from Danone. He was there for twenty years. He knew nothing about organic, nothing about sustainable packaging, nothing about environmental footprints and logistics, but this stuff gave new life to his career."[2]

Keith Tice was in charge of purchasing at his company, which was a chain of retail stores. When it came to buying environmentally superior products, he gave his purchasing agents leeway. They were allowed to collectively spend 5 percent more on environmentally superior products. If, for example, one item cost 10 percent more, it would be balanced by another item bought in the same quantity that was the same price as its environmentally inferior counterpart. Note: they never even came close to paying 5 percent more.

Look at your products' packaging. If you are a B2B operation and ship most packages to the same customers, consider using reusable, not throwaway, containers, especially if your own fleet delivers the products and returns empty back to your facility. Many companies are saving a lot of money by using reusable packaging.

Even if you are in consumer sales, consider reusable containers. Milk used to be delivered to homes in reusable bottles and the empty bottles were picked up. There was a steep deposit on the bottles. What customer loyalty that engendered!

Rule 6—Know Thy Suppliers

Being accused of employing sweatshop labor is something no company can afford to do any longer. Shunning manufacturers who use sweatshop labor began in 1996 with headlines that revealed that Kathie Lee Gifford's clothing collection was made in illegal sweatshops. With all the attention being paid to what you purchase as a sustainable enterprise, it's time to look at what your vendors purchase as well. For example, most companies ignore where their retirement dollars are invested. (Your vendor in this case is your retirement plan provider.) In many cases, employees' retirement dollars are invested in areas in conflict with their personal values. Social(k)[3] ensures that your retirement dollars are invested in socially responsible investments. Take a close look at where your retirement plan vendor is spending your dollars.

Much of the world is now importing from a sweatshop nation, China. Within the last two years, products have come from China with the following hidden "surprises":

- Melamine (a plastic that appears to be a protein in tests) in animal feed, pet food, dairy products, and infant formula
- Lead in the paint on kids' toys
- Propylene glycol in toothpaste
- Noxious sulfur-fume-emitting compounds in drywall sheet rock
- Illegal levels of antibiotics in farmed fish
- Heparin made from pig intestines in unsanitary kitchen sinks but certified as a USP (U.S. Pharmacopeia) grade pharmaceutical

People, including children and infants, and pets have died because of these products.

And the costs to the manufacturers who buy and resell these products from China and the retailers who sell them (such as product recall costs and product liability payments) are staggering. A friend's company that was importing certified organic food from China just went out of business when the USDA turned away the shipping containers because the "certified organic foods" registered off the scale on pesticides.

Know who makes your stuff. If you were buying it locally, of course you would visit the plant. If you are buying overseas to save money, use a fraction of the money you would save and go over and visit the plant. As an alternative, use a reputable third-party certifying organization. You have to be nuts to buy from an overseas source and not have third-party verification of the terms and conditions of the contract.

Just after the Tiananmen Square massacre, when China added a new layer of oppression on its people and a new opaque layer on its already closed practices, a brilliant, Chinese-speaking, African-American Harvard alum named Heather White discussed environmental audits with David as part of the emerging new field of social auditing.[4] She had the idea of using a social audit process to determine the veracity of Chinese product and manufacturing claims. She formed an organization called Verité.[5] Now, under the direction of Dan Viederman, Verité has programs in China, India, Southeast Asia, Bangladesh, Mexico, Latin America, and many other countries and regions. Verité inspects factories and monitors compliance with that country's laws as well as UN laws regarding human rights. It also audits for compliance with the contracts between manufacturers and their contracting companies.

Its customers include large companies such as the Gap, Levi Strauss, Timberland, Nautica, and New Balance and smaller companies such as Eileen Fisher. Other third-party organizations also validate contractual terms. These terms can go beyond environmental considerations and human rights.

We know many leaders of successful small businesses who go to the countries where their raw materials or products come from and not only conduct inspections but create wonderful empowering relationships with the producers and farmers to ensure that their products are organic and fair trade and made without violating human rights, such as Dean's Beans,[6] Theo Chocolate,[7] Bio Group International, and Kopali Organics, and they use these trips to maximum advantage in their product marketing. However, if you really cannot afford overseas trips to your major vendors, at least collaborate with other purchasers of products from the same facility or rely on third-party verification inspections.

If you are buying domestically, visit your major suppliers and periodically survey them on their sustainability attributes. It is good to capture their current sustainability practices on paper, and it always helps nudge them in the right direction when you ask them questions about their sustainability practices. (See the supplier questionnaire in resource H.)

Finding out about your suppliers' sustainability practices is no longer an optional activity if you want to remain competitive. Walmart has just launched a fifteen-question supplier sustainability questionnaire for its more than 100,000 worldwide suppliers of products.[8]

Rule 7—Embrace Standards, Screens, and Protocols

To ensure that you are buying products that are environmentally superior, socially responsible, and sustainable, *buy products and services that comply with one or more of the various green product standards* described in chapter 5, like Green Seal, TerraChoice, Blue Angel, Nordic Countries, NSF (formerly the National Sanitation Foundation), and Scientific Certification Systems. And if a standard does not exist, create your own, just like Paulette Mae Cole did.

We worked with Paulette, founder and CEO (creative energy officer) of ABC Home, who decided to transition her fashion-forward home furnishings company to become more sustainable. Paulette had gone to the big annual home furnishings shows, like High Point Market in North Carolina, and talked to all the manufacturers and vendors seeking furniture made from sustainable, responsibly harvested woods. They had no idea what she was talking about. Up to that point, sustainable certified woods were sourced only for construction of LEED certified buildings. The stakes were much higher in the furniture industry, where there was a customer premium on furniture made from exotic, rare, tropical woods. Unfortunately, customers weren't aware that much of this wood came from clear-cutting of old growth rain forests and resulted in not just the disappearance of exotic wood species but also a loss of habitat and endangered species.

Paulette hired Amy Chender, formerly with Riverkeeper, as director of social responsibility. Collaborating with the Rainforest Alliance, ABC Home created its own "goodwood" standard and label. The key component of the standard is that every piece of wood in goodwood labeled furniture has documentation tracing its pedigree back to the specific forest it came from. Only forests managed for sustainability can meet the standard. This involves third-party auditing from organizations like the Forest Stewardship Council, the Sustainable Forestry Initiative, Program for the Endorsement of Forest Certification, and Canadian Standards Association. In addition, for every goodwood labeled product ABC sells, ranging in price from a few dollars to a few thousand, a tree is planted. This planting program is under the direction of Dr. Wangari Maathai, the Kenyan environmental activist who won the 2004 Nobel Peace Prize for her contribution to sustainable development, democracy, and peace for the planting of millions of trees and creation of the African Greenbelt Movement. An ABC goodwood customer even gets certification for the carbon credits.

Paulette notes, "Customers come into ABC and are first seduced by the beauty of the products. Then they see the goodwood label and a whole customer education component takes place where they learn more about the wood sourcing and importance of using responsibly managed wood. Similarly with the vendors, the goodwood program educates the manufacturers on sustainability and is structured as a stepwise program so that vendors can make the transition to goodwood incrementally."[9]

Screens are tools that help identify and eliminate products or services with unwanted attributes. Daniel Siegel, who previously created the wildly successful Student Advantage affinity card, created the Evo Store[10] algorithm, which screens and compares consumer products based on an ever-expanding database of environmental and social attributes. While online shopping engines allow you to compare products based on price and performance features, the Evo Store algorithm examines over 10 million products' SKU data feeds to let you know if a toy is lead-free, a water bottle contains bisphenol-A, or a washing machine is water and energy efficient. These feeds contain a great deal of often buried but useful information about individual products such as where they're manufactured (e.g., made in the USA versus China), how they're manufactured (e.g., solar- or wind-powered factory), and what materials are used (e.g., organic cotton, recycled glass, bamboo). With these attributes defined, quantified, and weighted by experts such as David, Hunter Lovins, Karl Burkhart, Charlotte Stephenson, Wendy Gorden, and Seth Bauer, only 150,000 products (1.5 percent) of the 10 million tested have passed the rigorous "green screen." While the analysis relies on data provided by the manufacturers, the Web site is "policed" for fraud by allowing the community to find and flag discrepancies. The actual environmental data for each of the 10 million products can be viewed online as well.[11]

Companies use many different sustainability procurement protocols. For example, Patagonia is using a "no cotton" procurement protocol because of the environmental devastation created by traditional cotton farming. For example, cotton uses one-quarter of the pesticides in the United States and 2,800 gallons of water for one cotton bedsheet or 2,900 gallons of water for one pair of blue jeans.[12] Aveda adopted a "no petroleum-based ingredients" procurement policy. Most environmentally responsible publishers and printers refuse to use paper without at least 30 percent postconsumer waste recycled content. Made by indigenous people using indigenous ingredients, fair trade, and animal cruelty-free are other procurement protocols. Two procurement protocols that are discussed in some detail below are guidelines for organic foods and buying local.

As a follow-up to the story about Aveda's environmental audit and the missing 1.2 million pounds of organic ingredients, Horst continued the story:

> After Estée Lauder bought Aveda, I stayed on board in the transition. Leonard Lauder came over here to work with me for two years and really became an environmentalist and an environmental investor. At the time, a new director of environmental affairs and sustainability was put on who was not really an environmentalist but who was very politically adroit and popular with the environmental groups because of the strategic way she distributed Aveda's philanthropic contributions.
>
> In addition to petroleum-free, organic, and environmental responsibility, I also brought indigenous practice into Aveda. After buying into the organic in a big way, so its Origins line of products uses much more organic ingredients than we ever did, I introduced Estée Lauder to indigenous culture. We went to upstate New York to the Oneida Nation, and the head of the Lauder groups got very turned on and sympathetic and decided to come

out with a new product called Indigenous made with indigenous ingredients. The "treaty" we made was to give the profits to the indigenous peoples.

The product was a huge success and raised millions of dollars, but instead of giving the money to the indigenous peoples, the director of environmental affairs gave the money to the same environmental groups that she had given money to previously. The indigenous people felt cheated again by the white man and that the white man could not be trusted. I was horrified that this happened and resigned. The tribe testified against Aveda at the UN Permanent Forum on Indigenous Issues in May 2007 and then sued Aveda and won.[13]

Organic food is an area that has an extreme amount of interest, passion, politics, and misinformation. A review focusing on twelve relevant studies by researchers at the London School of Hygiene and Tropical Medicine and published in the *American Journal of Clinical Nutrition* showed that for ten out of thirteen food crops, organic food had no significant nutritional advantages over conventional food.[14] However, the parameters that were used in the review were the same parameters used in creation of the very political USDA Food Nutrition Labeling Program, which scores nutrition only as either protein, calories, fats, trans fat, salt, or fiber. Major classes of vitamins are required to be listed only if they are added ingredients.

So an organic fruit or vegetable with ten times more trace metals and vitamins as its conventional counterpart would be listed as having the same nutritional breakdown. This is clearly misleading and understating the value of organic food. One recent study showed that organic ketchup had 57 percent more lycopene, an antioxidant, than conventional ketchup.[15]

Lycopene is not part of the listed nutritional labeling required by the USDA.

The point is, organic food has real value and is a major factor in sustainability sourcing. The domestic market has hit about $25 billion and is growing at a 20 percent per annum rate. It is the only retail food market segment that is growing.

It is not just about nutrition but healthy pesticide- and herbicide-free food, healthy farmworkers, healthy soil, a healthy planet, and taste. While the Food and Drug Administration says that two-thirds of domestic and imported produce contains no pesticide residue, what about the other third? An analysis of 87,000 government tests by the Environmental Working Group[16] in a recent study showed that some fruits and vegetables have nine different pesticides in a single serving. The habitually worst ones are peaches, apples, bell peppers, celery, cherries, nectarines, strawberries, kale, lettuce, imported grapes, carrots, and pears.

When the USDA first promulgated standards for organic agriculture, the draft allowed foods to be labeled as organic if they were grown on sludge, irradiated, or genetically engineered. Over 275,000 Americans wrote in to protest and offered more sensible language to revise the draft standard. The current USDA National Organic Program standard[17] still has some weaknesses—such as allowing up to 5 percent nonorganic ingredients (excluding water and salt) in a product labeled as organic and not making a distinction between milk produced from cows that live on a factory farm and cows that graze in pastures on family farms.

One other important consideration in sustainability purchasing is buying local. A major battle is raging between thought leaders from both the organic side (championed by Whole Foods' John Mackey) and the local side (championed by Michael Pollan, author of *The Omnivore's Dilemma*). The argument is that an organic cucumber grown in South America and flown to the United States is neither fresh tasting nor environmentally superior to a locally grown cucumber, even if the local cucumber was grown with chemical fertilizers.

The buy-local argument also addresses issues of the huge environmental costs associated with transportation. Many countries of origin have very poor environmental practices, many of which have global implications, such as global warming.

Some recent studies tracking money flow[18] show that at national chain big-box retailers, like Walmart and Borders, approximately 86 percent of the money from purchases leaves the state, whereas with locally owned businesses, over 50 percent of the money stays local. If nothing but for purely selfish reasons, buying locally puts more money back into the local economy and thereby into your company's coffers. *The Small-Mart Revolution: How Local Businesses Are Beating the Global Competition* by Michael H. Shuman and other books make a very strong sustainability case for buying locally.

One organization whose mission is to aid and abet the development of local economies is the Business Alliance for Local Living Economies (BALLE).[19] Over 20,000 entrepreneurs are part of sixty-five local BALLE networks, which, among other things, helps their members buy locally.

"Be a Local Hero, Buy Local" is the signature slogan of Community Involved in Sustainable Agriculture.[20] This slogan inspired a wave of community supported agriculture groups (CSAs). Over 2,500 CSAs around the country are now included in Local Harvest's database,[21] such as Lancaster Farm Fresh Cooperative.[22] With a new slogan, "Buy Fresh, Buy Local," and a new champion, Michael Pollan, CSAs are thriving and are a great place to begin making your sustainable purchases if you use agricultural products in your business. Even national chains have jumped on the Buy Fresh, Buy Local bandwagon. For example, in 2006, Bon Appétit Management Company, with 400 locations in 29 states, spent $55 million in purchasing from 560 individual farms across the country.[23]

Rule 8—Use Purchasing Alliances

The basic purpose of most companies is to satisfy a need to inspire a purchase. It is truly rare that customers can't find anyone to take their money. Businesses can be very creative about figuring out ways of getting new customers and getting customers to give them money. In those rare circumstances where you cannot get a vendor to do exactly what you want, try forming a purchasing or contracting alliance. This is especially helpful if what you want requires that the vendor install capital equipment, use special ingredients, or otherwise spend more money to provide the product or service you want. In these cases, vendors can be motivated to make the change if you show them that the volume you will buy will justify making the change.

For example, Ben & Jerry's and Stonyfield Farm wanted to purchase rBGH-free milk exclusively from family farms, but individually, they didn't have enough buying power to demand this from their suppliers. Together they went to the St. Albans Cooperative Creamery and made a deal. The deal structure was essentially this: Ben & Jerry's and Stonyfield Farm will collectively buy about X pounds of milk per year. We will enter into an agreement with St. Albans to buy X pounds of rBGH-free milk per year with a Y cent per hundredweight premium.

Another example is the White Dog Cafe, a restaurant in Philadelphia known for its award-winning cuisine and social activism and founded by Judy Wicks. Its dishes are made from local organic foods, and the restaurant is carbon neutral. "We were the first restaurant in our area to buy electricity from renewable sources. In addition to rooftop solar panels, we also use the waste heat from our refrigeration system to preheat our hot water."[24] When Judy first went out to the local farming community to source organic pork and poultry that was not from a factory or any other farm that used gestational or battery cages and clipped chickens' beaks, she could not guarantee sufficient volume for the local producers to want to change their practices to get her business. So she created an alliance with her competitors. Judy got other restaurants in the Philadelphia area to form an alliance, and together they represented enough volume to get the producers to give them everything she wanted.

One of the largest purchasing alliances is the Western States Contracting Alliance (WSCA).[25] It is an alliance of the heads of the state procurement agencies of fifteen states— Alaska, Arizona, California, Colorado, Hawaii, Idaho, Minnesota, Montana, Nevada, New Mexico, Oregon, South Dakota, Utah, Washington, and Wyoming. One of its founders was our recently deceased friend Kitty Gillespie, formerly of the Washington Department of Ecology. According to WSCA's Web site, "All governmental entities within WSCA states as well as authorized governmental entities in non-WSCA states are welcome to use their approved agreements. Cooperative purchasing benefits states as well as cities, counties, public schools and institutions of higher education. Cooperative purchasing is effective and popular because it can save significant time and money in contract production as well as lower contract prices through the power of aggregation."

Aggregation works for collectives of nongovernmental purchasing agents as well. For green purchasing there is the International Green Purchasing Network.[26] Just one word of caution: when forming a procurement alliance, give some consideration to antitrust laws. Federal and state laws, like the

Sherman AntiTrust Law of 1890 and section 5 of the Federal Trade Commission's regulations, prohibit unfair competition.

Other resources are organizations whose raison d'être is to help connect green shoppers with green sellers, like Green America[27] (formerly Coop America). Green America is a national nonprofit consumer organization that promotes environmental sustainability and social and economic justice and is run by our friends Alisa Gravitz and Denise Hamler. Among its products are a National Green Pages directory and the Green Festival, showcasing green products approved by Green America.

Summary

When making purchasing decisions, remember these rules:

1. You are responsible for the environmental footprint of what you buy.

2. The customer is king or queen, and you, as a customer, have enormous power to influence the environmental practices of your vendors.

3. Ask your suppliers for green products and services. You should do business only with suppliers that appreciate the wake-up call you give them when you educate them on green products and services because even if you are the first to ask, rest assured that more and more customers will want green products in the future.

4. Write your green purchasing specifications on your purchase order form and prominently display them on your Web site and all correspondence. Your suppliers will assume then that they are not voluntary terms, but contractual obligations.

5. Empower your purchasing agents to buy green products and services. Include green purchasing as part of their performance evaluation and reward system.

6. Know thy suppliers. Make it your business to know the environmental practices of your suppliers. Use the vendor questionnaire in resource H to help you learn about your suppliers.

7. Embrace standards, screens, and protocols. Use existing environmental standards and protocols at least as guidance in making your purchasing decisions or create a standard if none exists.

8. Use purchasing alliances to help you identify environmentally superior products and vendors and to help reduce the cost of green purchasing.

This chapter dealt with using the power of your purse to reduce your impact on the environment. But to really reduce, you have to really reduce. The next chapter is a primer on how to reduce with a goal toward zero emissions and releases.

Reduce—
Getting to Net Zero
Emissions and Releases

This chapter is about voluntary commitments—going beyond government regulations—to making continuous improvement in reducing your total environmental footprint. Many companies and organizations are even making the commitment to reduce their emissions to air, releases to water, and solid waste to *zero*. It seems impossible to do and even more so to do it cost-effectively, yet all it takes is a voluntary commitment. The following examples show how it is done.

Net-zero-waste pioneer Gunter Pauli was CEO of Ecover, a small company that makes cleaning products (laundry powder, dishwashing liquid, car wax) from natural and renewable raw materials. Ecover opened a near-zero-emissions factory in Gunter's native Belgium in 1992. A grass roof kept the plant cool in summer and warm in winter. The water treatment system ran on wind and solar energy. The factory became a media darling. Ecover captured 6 percent of the Belgian detergent market in eighteen months without spending a dime on advertising. Gunter doesn't claim that zero emissions are cheaper, just that you make more money. David worked with him in the development of Gunter's Zero Emissions Research and Initiatives[1] pavilion for the 2000 Hannover World's Fair.

The Green Festival,[2] operated by Green America, conducts two-to-three-day festivals in five major U.S. cities with over 200,000 attendees. Denise Hamler and her crew of passionate volunteers recover 97 percent of their waste! For example, every food item, utensil (made from cornstarch), paper plate, cup, and napkin is composted.

David worked with a water-based-paint manufacturer after the company decided to go for zero releases to water. Once the decision was made, the creativity of the employees made all the rest possible. They switched all their ingredients to nontoxic materials, but the biggest step in getting to zero was that they changed the order in which they manufactured paint each day. They started the day manufacturing white and the lightest colors and moved to darker colors and then black at the end of the day. Because of this, they did not have to clean out the lines and vats between batch runs. When they washed out the lines at the end of the day, they put the wash water into a tank and flocculated it, letting the solids settle so that they could be dried and shipped to a landfill. Not only did the plant become a zero discharge facility, it saved money on chemical costs and sewer charges.

Industries in the Soviet Empire were responsible for incredible amounts of pollution. Just before its end, the Soviet regime enacted a regulation to reduce water pollution that was incredibly effective. Factories were required to discharge their effluents upstream from their freshwater intake. Pollution disappeared quickly.

The quickest and most cost-effective way of reducing to zero is to follow the rules described below.

Rule 1—Set a Target for Reduction

If you set a target for reduction, you are likely to hit it. For example, on dairy farms, water use can range from 12 to 150 gallons per cow per day.[3] What accounts for these huge differences has to do with whether anyone cares about how much water is used. Farms that meter their water use and set standards have very little water use compared to farms that don't. They set a target.

Another example is Stonyfield Farm, where Mission Action Program teams each have their own set of metrics targeted for reduction. Because of this, as Gary Hirshberg said, "The MAP teams are hacking away at the metrics."

One tip used by a lot of companies is for any operations requiring washing: use your last rinse water for your first wash water.

Rule 2—Measure and Publish Your Releases to Water, Emissions to Air, Solid Waste, and Recycling

If you can measure it, you can reduce it. To get to zero, look at your ten biggest emissions to air, your ten biggest releases to water, and your ten biggest solid waste items. (See chapters 2 and 4 for information on how to get these figures.) Identify where each item is coming from. Publish these numbers on your Web site, in your sustainability and annual reports, in your company newsletter, on CSRwire.com, on a poster in your break room, on the back of your purchase order forms, or in communications with customers. Then ask yourself these questions about each item: "I see how much I buy of each, but how much do I actually use?" "What would it take for me to discharge, emit, or throw out less or none of this?"

As for packaging material for the supplies that come to you regularly, ask your vendors and suppliers if these items can be delivered in reusable boxes, containers, or totes that you can send back to them for refilling when they are empty. At the same time, ask what kind of discount you will enjoy for reusing the containers instead of throwing them out.

Rule 3—Set Internal Standards as Benchmarks for Performance

How much water (hot and cold) does it take to make a batch? How much does it take to clean out the equipment? In chapter 7 we discussed reducing energy use by installing meters and programmable controls. The same holds true for your use of water and other raw materials. Put meters everywhere and assign every meter to someone who will be responsible for keeping track of the baseline and, over time, working to reduce the quantity of water or other material used per unit produced. Install flow restrictors in places where there is no benefit to an unrestricted flow, like bathroom sinks and toilets.

Pick the average performance as the standard and incrementally raise the bar over time. For example, if the worst individual performance in cleaning a vat is 250 gallons of water use, the best is 20 gallons, and the average is 80 gallons, set 80 as the standard. Naysayers will not be able to criticize because at least one employee can do it in 20. When you reset the standard (in no sooner than two years), the worst performance will be 80 and the best perhaps better than 20, thus increasing the standard for reduction.

Time needs to be factored into performance standards as well. The timely use of raw materials can make a difference in how efficiently they can be used. In farming, for example, about half of the nitrogen in chemical fertilizer makes it to the crop; the rest is lost to the environment, causing environmental problems like the great dead zones in the Gulf of Mexico and the Chesapeake Bay. If you apply manure fertilizer and wait just one week instead of immediately incorporating it into the soil, the amount of available nutrients for your crops drops from 75 percent to 15 percent.[4] In other words, wait one week and you waste 85 percent of the fertilizer you applied. Worse than waste, the wasted nutrients end up polluting downstream, as the nitrogen lost due to volatilization to the atmosphere eventually precipitates back to earth.

Rule 4—Improve Quality and Cleanliness

Defects are a major cause of waste in some industries. One way to reduce defects is to track the results of your quality control programs. Another way is to implement ISO 9000—the global total quality management standard. By improving quality, you will reduce defects and thereby reduce waste.

In the electronics semiconductor industry, for example, semiconductor chips are made by drawing a circuit diagram and photoreducing it onto a semiconducting material. As semiconductor chips got smaller, dust began to have a huge impact by causing defects. At this point, the ability to further miniaturize has mostly to do with the ability to create ever-cleaner environments.

In most companies, cleanliness has a lot to do with yields and QC rejects. Cleanliness may or may not be next to godliness, but it's right on top of profitability. Stonyfield Farm uses live cultures in making its yogurt. Imagine what could happen if these cultures got contaminated. The company's manufacturing facility looks almost like a semiconductor clean room or hospital operating theater. It even has clean stations to ensure that shoes get disinfected before people move from one room to another.

In the most tragic example of poor sanitation, product contamination at a well-respected beverage company making juice from natural products ended the life of a young child. Afterward the company added a step to its manufacturing process

to ensure aseptic operations. In another example of tragic possibilities, at a high-technology company, David witnessed large
amounts of radioactive waste merely cordoned off with clear
vinyl sheeting sealed with duct tape.

Rule 5—Dewater and Treat Your Wastewater

Do you have an effluent that contains particulates or solids?
Consider dewatering it. A variety of technologies, including
centrifuges, belt filters, screw presses, decanters, cyclone sepa-
rators, and settling ponds and tanks, can help you separate the
wastewater from the solids.

If the wastewater gets cleaned enough in this process,
perhaps it can be used for some other purpose or directed to
an artificial wetland that mimics nature's methods of purifying water. Or perhaps the liquid can undergo reverse osmosis
(RO). RO is a process where pressure is applied to a liquid so
that the liquid goes through a semipermeable membrane but
the dissolved solids do not. RO is used for detoxifying blood
in kidney dialysis, making maple syrup and fruit concentrates,
and purifying drinking water and water for specialty applications (including car wash rinse water). RO can, for example,
take up to 95 percent of the pollutants out of the water and
move them to 20 percent of the water, so that 80 percent of the
water has only 5 percent of the pollutants it originally had. Not
good enough? You can run it through more RO cycles until you
get the water quality you want.

If the solids content of this treated wastewater is too high to
run through RO or an artificial wetland, you can treat it biologically in an anaerobic (no-oxygen) process and aerobic (oxygen-
rich) process or with a microaerobic anoxic (very little oxygen)
process. In aerobic processes, biological and chemical oxygen

demand is reduced sometimes to nothing. In microaerobic processes, nutrients are biologically converted to inert form (like ammonia into inert nitrogen gas) or biologically sequestered.

The organic content of liquid waste streams can also be treated using anaerobic digestion to produce biogas that contains methane and is flammable. You can then buy an electrical generator that runs on this gas. Stonyfield generates waste yogurt in plastic containers resulting from quality control rejects and statistical quality control sampling of products. It now has a machine that separates the yogurt from the plastic containers so the yogurt can be anaerobically digested and made into gas, which is used to run the plant. Gary Hirshberg recalled, "The water treatment engineers who worked for us used to believe that 'the solution to pollution is dilution.' And then we built a wastewater treatment plant that produced methane and less sludge, and we made money."[5]

Fish farming has become one of the major sources of water pollution in the world. At Australis, where barramundi fish are raised indoors, Josh Goldman said, "We recycle our water sixty times per day and treat it without the use of chemicals, dewater it, and produce an organic fertilizer, which we provide to local farmers twice per year who immediately incorporate it into their soil, eliminating any polluting environmental footprint we might have."[6]

Anaerobic digestion does not deal with the ammonia nitrogen or phosphorus pollutants in the water, so Australis took water treatment an additional step. Its wastewater goes through a denitrification process that converts the ammonia to nitrate and then converts the nitrate into nitrogen gas, which is what 80 percent of the earth's atmosphere is made of.

If you dewater organic material to greater than 25 percent solids, you can compost the solids. Composting is a biological process mimicking what happens on the forest floor. In essence, the organic materials undergo decay. According to the EPA's Process to Further Reduce Pathogens (PFRP) and Vector Attraction Reduction (VAR),[7] composting can convert material that would have to be sent to a landfill into a usable soil amendment. When composting, it is important to have a six to one carbon-to-nitrogen ratio of the starting materials because the compost will produce (outgas) ammonia if the nitrogen content is too high or will produce methane and VOCs if the carbon content is too high. You can, for example, put corrugated cardboard or newspaper (which is low in nitrogen) in the compost if the nitrogen content is too high. Compost yard waste, foodstuffs, coffee grounds, tea bags, and paper napkins, plates, and tissues from your office and use the material for the indoor plants, giving oxygen to your office space, reducing Dumpster fees and energy use for transport of waste to the landfill, and reducing the burden on landfills.

Windrow composting is the most common form of composting. Long rows of organic material approximately 8 feet tall are set in a field and the rows are mixed frequently, so that what is inside gets to the outside and is exposed to air. Windrow composting, however, is no longer legal in Southern California because the material inside is underoxygenated and undergoes anaerobic decomposition, resulting in emissions of ammonia and VOCs. Composting with pressurized air forced though the compost pile has been shown to be effective in producing composts with 80 percent lower ammonia and VOC outputs than for windrow composting. If the process is done well, the starting material can get composted down to almost nothing—only carbon dioxide, nitrogen gas, water vapor, and a very little bit of solids.

Alternatively, you can dry your dewatered organic solids further and use them as a fuel. For a long time, pulp mills have been powered by combustion of dried organic solids.

The costs to dewater and treat wastewater vary greatly based on the compounds present, the consistency, and the dilutions. Our friend Dr. James Morris has designed wastewater treatment facilities ranging from a system he developed for Tom's of Maine that treated a very clean (and minty fresh) waste stream to systems for waste streams with dilutions of, for example, 10 milligrams per liter of nitrogen and waste streams that are 10 percent solid, such as livestock manure. In wastewater treatment, whether the influent is sewage, livestock waste, or waste from a manufacturing or processing plant or cleaning operation, a primary treatment process removes as many of the solids as possible, and a secondary treatment process substantially degrades the biological content of the sewage that is derived from human waste, food waste, soap, and detergent.

The average person produces about 9 pounds of nitrogen and 1 pound of phosphorus waste in his or her urine each year. A recent study of all the wastewater treatment facilities in Pennsylvania showed that it costs up to $250 per pound in some treatment plants to remove nitrogen.[8] On the other hand, you can buy nitrogen and phosphorus credits from companies like Red Barn Trading Company[9] for $10 per pound. So, in looking at the costs to treat water and mitigate nitrogen and phosphorus pollution, see how cost-effectively you can treat your waste stream. If you can't treat it for less than $10 per pound, buy credits. They have the same benefit to the environment as treating your wastewater yourself. And if you can mitigate nitrogen and phosphorous for less than $10 per pound, do so and register and then sell your credits to pay for your treatment system.

Rule 6—Reuse Your Gray Water, Treated Wastewater, Solvents, and Oils

The rainwater you collect from your roof and other gray water that your facility produces can be stored and later used to water plants, or it can be sand filtered and used to flush toilets. Wastewater can be treated with reverse osmosis, and the purified portion can be used for nonpotable water uses.

In the previous section, we gave you the basic recipe for separating the water from the solids in your effluent and wet organic waste so that the water can be reused or recycled and the solids composted and used as a soil amendment or burned as a fuel. These processes also produce saleable carbon and nutrient credits. Here are some tips for reusing solvents and oils:

- If you buy and use solvents and then have to pay to dispose of the used solvents, consider installing vacuum distillation equipment to clean and recover your solvents.

- If you extract vegetable oil from feedstock, consider that yields using solvent extraction methods are frequently twice as high as expeller (mechanical squeezing) methods. With solvent extraction, you can even choose plant-based solvents and can use vacuum distillation equipment to clean and recover the solvents.

- If your facility uses any petrochemical product, a NASA spinoff bioremediation product has been developed by Universal Remediation[10] that can capture oil or gas spilled on the ground or be spread over the affected area. Microbes eat the oil and produce compost. The return on investment for this product has inspired Joe to use it at Gasoline Alley. Once the gas and oil is eaten, the remains are thrown in the gardens.

Rule 7—Don't Emit Your Products or Waste Products into the Air

The atmosphere is not your private profit center.

In keeping with the principle of conservation of matter, a particular waste can manifest itself as a release to water, an emission to air, or a solid waste. When town dumps started to fill up—and worse, leach pollutants into the water table and aquifers—ingenious planners thought of incinerating the waste. If you had 100 tons of waste and you incinerated it, you might end up with only 10 tons of ash. Magic. Where did the other 90 tons go? Up into the air, of course, but some of it precipitated back to earth onto someone else's property, and some of that reentered the water supply. It turned out that incineration was not an environmental solution. It's just a way of turning your problem into someone else's problem. You used to be able to solve the problem of releases to water by just converting them into emissions to air. EPA has wised up to this trick and has tried to work within the constraints of the Clean Water Act and the Clean Air Act to regulate across media (solids, liquid, and gas from the same source simultaneously).

However, this book is not about regulatory compliance but voluntary compliance with your highest principles. Doing the right thing in the context of air emissions is not having emissions to air different than the constituents of air.

If you have unregulated emissions but still have NO_x or SO_x (sulfur oxide) in your emissions to air, consider using a selective catalytic reduction (SCR) system that injects ammonia into the stack gases. NO_x is produced in every combustion process; the hotter the combustion temperature, the more NO_x created. You can get rid of the NO_x using catalytic converters or the SCR process. SO_x on the other hand, can be produced only if the fuel you are combusting contains sulfur. Low-sulfur fuel produces low-sulfur emissions. To avoid SO_x emissions, therefore, you can pick low-sulfur fuels, treat the sulfur in the smokestack, or remove the sulfur from the fuel before burning it. The process of integrated gasification combined cycles converts coal into a gas and removes the sulfur before the gas is burned.

The best way to get rid of polluting emissions is to require companies to quantify them and publish the results. While U.S. laws were lax in actually proscribing emissions to air (and releases to water), the Toxic Release Inventory (TRI) under section 313 of the Emergency Planning and Community Right-to-Know Act (EPCRA 313) required the reporting of your emissions and releases of 650 specific toxic chemicals[11] above a certain quantity for businesses that have ten or more full-time employees and that fit within a specific NAICS (North American Industry Classification System) code. Approximately 1,300 companies required by law to file a TRI joined a program called the EPA 33/50 Program. In this program, some of the biggest polluting companies in the country, once forced to publish their toxic releases, reduced their pollution of 17 priority chemicals by between 33 percent and 50 percent.

Again, if you have compliance requirements, we are assuming that you are meeting them. If you don't have compliance requirements, do it anyway.

Every company is required to have a loose-leaf binder containing the Material Safety Data Sheets (MSDSs) of all the chemicals it uses. First, make sure your binder is complete, accurate, and current. Mark as obsolete and file away old MSDS sheets after you make sure you have the current ones. The MSDS binder is for your and your employees' protection. In the event of a chemical spill or if some chemical splatters into someone's face, you don't want to go running around looking for your MSDS binder and then trying to figure out which of the many seemingly duplicate documents you have is the one to follow for remediation procedures.

Second, go through your MSDS binder to see which chemicals you have are listed as toxic under EPCRA 313. Make a list of all the chemicals and list what quantity you use per year. Third, publish this list as widely as you can. Put it on your bulletin board. Put it on your Web site. Publish it in your annual stakeholder report. At the top say, "This is a list of chemicals as well as the quantities we used last year that the federal government has listed as toxic and hazardous." With proper attention, the list should decrease each year.

Do you think that we are asking the impossible of you? You might be saying, "My company is too small for all this attention." When Joe owned a small soda company, he implemented many of these examples and moved beyond the regulatory requirements. When it came time for Lipton Ice Tea and Sunkist Orange Soda to select a regional manufacturing plant, they selected his. This decision dramatically increased sales and attracted the attention of other opportunities and partnerships.

Some companies' operations emit dust. Even sewing machines produce airborne lint when the needles pierce a fabric. Some companies making clothes have sewing machines that vacuum the air at the point of contact between the needle and the cloth and send it to a filter. If you produce particulate matter, dust, or lint over a certain threshold, you are required to install a baghouse—a series of filters capturing the particulates. But even if you don't exceed the threshold, there is nothing to stop you from installing a baghouse or other means of capturing airborne particulates and dust generated from your operations.

If your operation involves repeatedly cutting or shredding anything such as wood, cloth, paper, tires, concrete, plastic, or glass, look into technologies to mitigate the production of airborne particles. Particulate matter is also created chemically—for instance, in the reaction of ammonia and NO_x. Look into the use of stand-alone electrostatic cleaners, negative ion generators, or high-efficiency particulate arrestor (HEPA) or submicron air filters or having these installed in your HVAC system as a way of reducing airborne particulate emissions.

At one time, Joe owned an air filtration equipment company. Exercising innovation, he created a number of business opportunities by exposing the risks associated with airborne particulates to potential clients. Once he identified a situation that needed attention (in one example, he demonstrated the risks of airborne formaldehyde in the embalming process in funeral homes), he created a business unit and sold quite a few HEPA air filtration systems. In the same way, strategies for sustaining your own business operations become new business opportunities for yourself and others.

Rule 8—Reduce Solid Waste Through Smarter Consumption

A lot of what we've discussed so far are "end-of-pipe" solutions. But there are a host of "beginning-of-pipe" solutions, or methods of reducing pollution by reducing consumption.

We came across an all-you-can-eat sushi bar that created a brilliant way to smartly reduce consumption. It charged customers for any food left on their plates. Other restaurants are offering fantastic specials that you can get only if you preorder them one or two days in advance. Think about just-in-time and other ways to buy only what you need to save money and reduce waste.

As discussed in chapter 5 on green design, people don't really want a ¼-inch drill bit. They want a ¼-inch hole. What is your real business? What is the *result* your customer wants accomplished?

In the mail-order business, a company's or organization's goal is not to send out the most mailings at the lowest price per mailing. Its goal is to get new customers or members at the lowest cost per acquisition. Rethinking your business in this context generally translates to reductions in waste.

Rule 9—Reuse Whatever You Can

Once an item is manufactured, the longer it lasts, generally the lower its environmental impact. One of the parameters of sustainability is durability. If two vehicles have equal miles-per-gallon ratings but one will last for 100,000 miles and the other 200,000, the one that lasts twice as long generally will have a significantly smaller environmental footprint. Paying 20 percent more for a car or truck tire that lasts twice as long is a good economic and sustainable choice. Whether drill bits and machine tools, manufacturing equipment, or office equipment, buy stuff that is durable so that your cost per year is optimized and your environmental footprint is minimized.

Durability provides for maximizing reuse. As mentioned previously, if you ship to the same customers and receive materials from the same customers, consider investing in reusable shipping containers, from shoebox size cartons to 1-ton totes. You will help the planet and definitely save money.

Eileen Fisher designs and manufactures sophisticated clothing for fashion-conscious professional women. Its garments are increasingly made using sustainable materials and low-impact dyeing processes, and its factories are audited against the Social Accountability International SA 8000 social standard with third-party verification. It recently opened up a unique lab store that sells new and used Eileen Fisher clothing. A reuse program allows customers to return their worn garments. The good-quality returns and samples are then cleaned and refurbished and sold for a fraction of the original price. The profits from the used clothing sales support charitable organizations through the company's grant-making program. What a brilliant way to add new brand-loyal customers at a lower price point while becoming more sustainable by minimizing waste.

TerraCycle makes all of its products from someone else's waste. It recently started packaging one of its products, a fertilizer made from liquefied castings from worms fed only organic food waste, in used soda bottles. This is the first product to receive the Zerofootprint seal for products that have virtually no negative environmental repercussions.[12]

Rule 10—Recycle and Group the Recyclables

The next chapter deals with using your waste as a feedstock—the ultimate recycling. This section deals with the collection side of the recycling equation. There was a time when employees had a wastebasket under their desk or at their workstation. Then small recycling containers started to be placed next to it. At that time, one often heard reports of the maintenance staff "cheating" by combining the waste from both bins when they were emptied at night, but nonetheless, people began recycling. Then some companies started to put a large recycling container under the desk and a very small waste container. This seemed to work: the smaller the trash container, the more recyclables collected.

In recycling, the more groupings of recyclables, the more valuable the sorted materials. For example, some recycling receptacles encourage the comingling of used office paper, newspapers, magazines, cardboard, and corrugated paper. However, if you separate these materials, they have more value. Are you sorting your solid waste into like groupings? Also, the more recycled material you have in a single category (paper, glass, etc.), the more valuable it is.

In our area, Eric Weiss, chair of the Pioneer Valley Sustainability Network, championed the creation of the Springfield Materials Recycling Facility,[13] which serves 1 million people in seventy-eight municipalities. It covers the largest geographic area of any single recycling operation in the country. Instead of collectively spending $6 million in tipping charges, these seventy-eight municipalities have their recyclables picked up for no charge—and they receive $1 million for the sale of these materials.

Current prices, down 20–50 percent from before the economic downturn of 2008–2009, are about $1,000 per ton for aluminum, $340 per ton for plastic, $276 per ton for glass, and $126 per ton for paper. No matter how you look at it, recycling makes economic sense. Springfield owns the facility and has been recognized for its leadership in this project, which made it one of the top five green cities in America.[14] The facility is operated by Waste Management Inc.,[15] which processes waste for 20 million customers in the country.

Joe runs CSRwire.com from the offices of the Gasoline Alley Foundation in Springfield. Every day, men push their shopping carts filled with bottles, cans, and metals—anything they can recycle—up the street to recycling facilities. Many of these aspiring entrepreneurs have graduated from shopping carts to small vans and ultimately trucks to collect materials for recycling. From homelessness on the street to a sustainable business with independent living, the recycling business sustains new life.

Some municipalities now even have curbside compost pickup. If you don't compost on-site you can have food waste; paper napkins, towels, and facial tissue; and grass and yard clippings comingled and composted. Some municipalities pay for the organic material they receive to compost (because it is cheaper to compost than to dispose of in a landfill site). Some municipalities sell or give away the compost they create. Joe has filled his property and grown hundreds of plants with the Springfield compost.

Look at the quantity of cellulosic material (wood, paper, corrugated paper, lint, and rags [cotton and linen]) you can recover from your waste. Consider using this as a solid fuel. It could be both the economically viable and environmentally superior choice. The weight of wood per cord (128 cubic feet) varies but is about 2 tons per cord. If you can get $126 per ton for used paper, that is the equivalent of approximately $250 per cord. If you can get wood for less than $250 per cord, then sell the paper for recycling, but if you can't get that price for the paper or if cordwood costs more, burn the paper in your solid fuel furnace. Anything that you burn as fuel that comes from plant material within the last few hundred years is considered carbon neutral for purposes of calculating the impact on global warming and has pretty much the same Btu per dry pound as wood. In this way, Waste Management produces power for 1 million people from waste it cleanly burns. Joe burns discarded wood pallets to heat a building that's used to help sustainable entrepreneurs get started.

Make sure you recycle your used office equipment (computers, printers, monitors, etc.). About 70 percent of the heavy metals in landfills comes from discarded electronics.[16] In 2005 about 2.2 million tons of electronics became obsolete, yet 1.8 million tons were disposed of and only 0.4 million tons were recycled—about 18 percent.[17] Don't know where to recycle your electronics? Plug into the EPA's eCycling campaign.[18]

Actually, is there anything you have and use in quantity that can't be recycled? Pallets? Used office furniture? Fry oil?

Lubricants? The key to successful recycling is offering whatever you are recycling in quantity and relatively clean. Find a home for everything you have that you don't use. You may even be able to sell it on Craigslist or to donate it and get a tax deduction.

For example, Rhino Records built its record label on selling recycled hits—songs that used to be number one that no one wanted anymore. In the recording industry, a large number of records are produced, packaged, and shipped in hopes that one will be a hit. For every hit there are too many misses that end up discarded. Rhino's oldies are goldies.

Summary

This chapter presented a number of examples of zero waste initiatives that illustrate a competitive advantage, promote positive public relations, raise awareness for your company, and create business opportunities for yourself and others. Companies that succeeded at reducing cost-effectively, such as Ecover, Green Festival, and Stonyfield Farm, all created metrics targeting reduction techniques. Remember these rules to successfully reduce, reuse, and recycle:

1. Set a target for reduction. You are likely to hit it.

2. Measure and publish your releases to water, emissions to air, solid waste, and recycling.

3. Set standards as benchmarks for performance.

4. Improve production quality and cleanliness. Reducing defects and waste saves money.

5. Dewater and treat your wastewater.

6. Reuse your gray water, treated wastewater, solvents, and oils.

7. Don't emit your products or waste products into the air.

8. Reduce solid waste through smarter consumption.

9. Reuse whatever you can.

10. Recycle and group the recyclables. The more groupings of recyclables, the more valuable the sorted materials— and the better the recycling infrastructure to receive the material.

The next chapter will build on the idea of reduction of waste as a solution for turning an environmental problem into a business opportunity. Giving value to that which has been abandoned is the ultimate sustainable enterprise.

Waste—
Turning an Environmental
Problem into a
Business Opportunity

This final chapter is about Joe's favorite topic and about the ultimate in being sustainable; instead of using resources and producing waste, using waste to produce resources. Sustainable businesses are popping up all over that are making money by turning an environmental problem into a business opportunity. In the United States, we create a lot of waste. This waste can be repurposed into something useful to create jobs, sustain the environment, and inspire innovation.

Living creatures spend most of their time finding and eating food. A creature that finds a food source that no other species is using is defined as its own species and guaranteed survival. That is one of the reasons why in nature, every creature's waste is another creature's food.

Life has been on this planet for approximately 3.5 billion years. With an estimated annual biomass production of approximately 200 gigatons,[1] if all creatures' waste was not eaten by other creatures and recycled, the entire surface of the earth would be covered in excrement approximately 700 miles thick.

It's impossible to be sustainable without using other creatures' wastes as your raw materials. In our unsustainable recent past, things were made with whatever was cheap and abundant.

Oil, coal, and natural gas were cheap and abundant, so pretty much every chemical was made from them.

This is why architect and designer William McDonough refuses to use the term "cradle to grave" in life cycle analysis and designs with a cradle-to-cradle approach. He and Michael Braungart designed a series of textiles in a full palette of colors that are ultimately "edible" in that the products, once they have completed their intended use, can be used as a feedstock or raw material for another process.

In manufacturing, the cost components are fairly equal for all manufacturers in the same product category. Facility costs, capital equipment costs, labor costs, energy costs, and raw material costs are generally the same from company to company in one product category. So, the company that can reduce its material costs relative to the competition wins.

For example, 100 years ago Henry Ford gave specifications for the wood crates in which his suppliers would ship parts to his factory. After uncrating, Ford disassembled the crates and used the precut wood pieces as parts in the car bodies. The remaining wood scraps were made into charcoal and sold under the Kingsford brand name, still a leading manufacturer of charcoal. Converting waste into a raw material made economic sense then and now.

Recycling Waste

Smart businesses use someone else's waste as their raw material, and the purer the waste stream, the higher its value as a raw material. With the development of automated sorting centers, a large variety of pure raw materials are available.

Huge amounts of recycled and recyclable materials are available to replace your business's raw materials. Not only are some companies getting good at sourcing recycled material, they are getting good at making continuous progress in getting it cheaper and purer.

The cleverest of companies go after the purest forms of discarded materials to use as raw materials to make their products. For example, biaxially oriented plastic resin is what is used to make shrink-wrap. It's so strong that a 1/1,000-inch film can hold over a ton of products together on a pallet. The resin costs up to $1 per pound. Waste shrink-wrap at home is comingled with other waste and no recycling infrastructure exists for it, but if you access the waste stream at a company that receives palletized goods, you can get used shrink-wrap in a largely uncontaminated pure form. Several companies use this superstrong, expensive polymer, which they get practically for nothing, to manufacture their products.

In the same way, Recycline takes the plastic lids that customers send back to Stonyfield Farm and converts the resin into toothbrushes. Metal Wood Common Good on Gasoline Alley in Springfield, Massachusetts, retrieves abandoned building materials and creates custom high-end furniture (basically, a zero-cost-of-goods process). IceStone in the Brooklyn Navy Yard uses crushed glass as the principal material in its beautiful countertops, which are environmentally superior alternatives to Formica or to quarried, cut, and polished stone.

One company David worked with had a brilliant business model. With only a small warehouse, a front-end loader, a desk, a chair, and a telephone, the company was given or bought for pennies on the dollar out-of-date-code Oreos, matzoh, Twinkies, breakfast cereal, and other long-shelf-life foods. It would blend them together, supplementing the mixture with vitamins and protein sources like soybeans, to make and sell hog feed meeting exacting specifications for nutrition. This client became a multimillionaire by "mining," repurposing, and selling refuse as a value-added product.

One of the cleverest recyclers is Julie Lewis. When other little girls were playing with dolls, she was playing with garbage. She created a line of shoes called Deja Shoe that transformed the industry. Many shoe companies now copy her approach to material reuse. The soles for her shoes were made from recycled car tires and cork, sourced from decorked wine bottles at Portland area restaurants. She set up recycling programs at schools to collect pen barrels and used them to manufacture the midsoles. The foam from discarded seat cushions was used in the tongues, and the uppers were made from the trim from disposable diapers, PET (polyethylene terephthalate) bottles, hemp, and discarded jeans. The logo on the shoe was made from recycled milk jugs. All in all she used twenty-two different waste materials in the manufacture of her shoes.[2]

All of this was great for marketing, and it even got her on *Oprah*, but to Julie it wasn't about marketing. In nature, one creature's waste is another creature's food. In traditional business, waste is stuff whose raw materials you had to pay for and use energy and labor to assemble and then you have to pay to get rid of it. Reduced cost of goods means more profit.

Deja Shoe was eventually sold. So what's Julie doing now? She recycled the name "Deja" into "Jade" and is working on a shoe made from recycled materials that uses the energy from each footstep to "inhale"—pump in air and sequester the excess carbon dioxide from the atmosphere. She is also making products like pocketbooks from old 35-millimeter film, purses from soda can pop tops, and pocketbooks and knapsacks from old PVC (polyvinyl chloride) lottery and advertising banners. Go, Julie!

Even the ultimate human waste, excrement, has value as a raw material. One company's product, Milorganite, is a premium fertilizer sold as a retail consumer product. It is made from human excrement processed at a wastewater treatment plant. The methane gas produced from the sewage treatment is even used in drying the fertilizer.

For years, companies made money mining bird and bat waste to be used as fertilizer and ingredients for detergent. Bion Environmental Technologies[3] built a company around mitigating the environmental footprint of livestock waste. Agricultural runoff is the number one water pollution in America, according to the EPA, and livestock waste is also a major source of air pollution. Bion's process squeezes the liquid out of cow manure, producing a hemicellulosic material that has the same energy content as wood per pound. In a clever eco-industrial manufacturing loop, the dewatered manure is combusted to power a corn-to-ethanol process.

Instead of feeding whole corn to cows, the cornstarch portion is fermented into alcohol and the wet distillers grain from the ethanol process is fed to the cows, which can't digest the cornstarch in the corn anyway. This process saves the equivalent of over 40,000 Btu of natural gas per gallon of ethanol, which has only 76,000 Btu per gallon. This process also produces tradable nutrient and carbon credits. The value of these credits is more than enough to pay for the installation of this technology.

Other companies such as Mascoma, Masada Range Fuels, and Lanza are making ethanol directly from the chemically or biologically digestible portions of garbage. One company, Qteros, is leveraging evolutionary biology and has found a microorganism that digests cellulose. This company has developed a microbe with a chemistry similar to that of termites that can eat sawdust and excrete ethanol. Qteros has even taken the reuse of human waste one step further. With its Q microbe, which converts cellulose into ethanol, it converts the cellulosic content of human sewage (which is responsible for biological and chemical oxygen demand in sewage treatment plants) to ethanol fuel.

Companies such as Honeywell UOP, Byogy, Delta Energy, and Sustainable Power have developed pyrolytic processes using temperature, pressure, and catalysts to convert organic material directly into an oil that can be refined into gasoline, aviation fuel, or diesel. While a bushel of soybeans will yield 20 percent biodiesel, that same bushel of soybeans in one of these processes will yield about 50 percent biodiesel, 25 percent flammable gas, and 25 percent char. But these processes will also make fuel from sawdust, crop waste, or even municipal waste consisting of paper, plastic, tires, and food waste. Similarly, Jason Tankersley at Waste Technology Transfer is taking cellulose in a bioliquefaction process and converting it into a high-Btu liquid fuel.

Instead of paying a tipping charge to throw something out, some companies are getting money to receive waste that they then remanufacture into new products. Depending on the material and the location, tipping charges run up to $125 per ton. The math on this is great. These companies are making money by

- Receiving tipping charges
- Not paying for raw materials
- Paying less to process materials (such as aluminum)
- Getting an increased market share by distinguishing the product as made from reclaimed materials
- Getting environmental credits (emissions credits, carbon credits, nutrient credits)

Another great example is Lancaster County's waste-to-energy facility in Pennsylvania. It's one of 100 facilities that burn municipal solid waste to make steam to run turbines. Trucks line up to enter the facility and dump their loads of trash. A crane picks up the waste and dumps it down a long shaft. At the bottom is a flameproof conveyor belt. The material burns on the belt, the ash falling through, and the metal is recovered at the end. At the back end are all manner of pollution control devices and baghouses to ensure that the emissions from this facility are largely just water and carbon dioxide. The ash goes to the landfill and the scrap metal is sold. Revenues come from the sale of electricity and tipping charges. Every truck is weighed coming in and going out, and the difference is assessed at $60 per ton. The facility also earns federal production tax credits for producing renewable energy. It's a sweet, sustainable business.

So, one way to make your company more sustainable is to examine your input materials and see if you could use someone else's output (waste) as your input. Can you make your product from recycled aluminum cans or from green, brown, or clear glass from glass bottles? What about using the bottles cut in half and fire-polished to make drinking glasses or using them as light conduits and insulation in a bottle house? How about PET, HDPE (high-density polyethylene), polypropylene from plastic bottles, paper, or cardboard? Is there something someone throws out regularly and in quantity that you can use to make your products?

Can you use your customers' waste as part of your raw materials stream? Aaron Lamstein built Worldwise, Inc., which "innovatively uses recycled resources and fashions them into high-quality pet products available at more than 30,000 leading retail stores throughout North America."[4] Its products include pet blankets made from recycled PET soda bottles. Similarly, Jason Tankersley is working with Beyer Block in using waste plastics that are not part of the plastics recycle commodity chain (plastic shopping bags) mixed with wood scraps to manufacture building blocks.

David visited the Fort Howard Paper Company in Wisconsin. All of its paper towel and tissue products are made from 100 percent postconsumer waste. Garbage trucks come in, and the material is sorted into piles of usable materials, including the fiber needed to make tissue and paper products. The company is very proud of its plant and offers tours. One tour consisted of a group of bankers. Walking through the facility, the tour guide grabbed a piece of used office paper from the pile waiting to be recycled and handed it to one of the bankers. Unfortunately, he happened to be the president of the bank where the paper had originated and it had confidential client information on it. Oh well.

If you start your business around the clever use of a material or item that no one wants, make sure the item that no one wants is an item you can reuse. One company David worked with is in the business of manufacturing soaps, hand cleaners, and hand lotions for institutions, shops and garages, and manufacturing facilities. It also provides the soap/lotion dispensers. At a deep discount, the company bought the entire dispenser inventory of another manufacturer that went out of business—25,000 dispensers. However, when workers began to install the dispensers, they got complaints. Janitors did not like them because they had to be turned upside down to be filled. Unless they were completely empty, the remaining contents ended up making a gloppy mess on the floor.

The company went to work to figure out what to do to salvage the use of these 25,000 brand-new dispensers. After an internal team spent a few years on the project with no success, they hired David. He took one look at the dispenser and came up with the idea of a standpipe/snorkel. It took David only thirty minutes of shop time to build the prototype. The plant manager looked at the device, rubbed his chin, and then had David follow him into the warehouse. The racks of shelves that housed the 25,000 dispensers had smaller boxes on the top shelves. The plant manager put up a ladder, climbed to the top, removed one of several thousand identical smaller boxes, took it down, opened it up, and removed a standpipe/snorkel virtually identical to the one David had made and said, "Oh, so that's what those things were for." Apparently the company had bought the solution along with the dispensers and just did not know it had it.

The ultimate waste feedstock is your business's own waste. For years Xerox was scolded by the environmental community for not refilling its disposable toner cartridges for its copy machines and laser printers. Finally it relented and built a facility to refill used Xerox toner cartridges. The facility cost around $10 million and the company assigned the costs to its public relations budget because it was thought of mainly as a way to promote the company's positive social attributes. To the company leaders' surprise, that one-time $10 million cost was responsible for annual profits in the hundreds of millions simply from refilling used cartridges instead of disposing of them and making new ones.

Interface Inc. makes its carpeting from used carpeting. When workers install new carpeting, they remove the customer's old carpeting and remanufacture it into the carpeting for the next customer. The company calculated that it has avoided $372 million in waste costs from 1995 to 2007, reduced its energy use by 45 percent since 1996, diverted 100 million pounds of material from landfills, and sold over 50 million square yards of climate neutral carpeting.

Safety-Kleen picks up hazardous and toxic material from companies and sells it back to them as new products. Every year the company picks up 400 million gallons of industrial waste and turns it into 300 million gallons of products.

TriState Biodiesel is among a growing group of companies that takes used vegetable oil or fat and makes it into a carbon neutral fuel that can be blended with diesel fuel or heating oil.

Finding New Business Opportunities

If you are thinking of starting a business or adjusting your existing enterprise, think about something someone throws out consistently and what you can make out of it. A variety of Web sites exist where people post information on their material needs and material surpluses. Check out what is available in quantity. Research the steps needed to create the infrastructure to collect it in a way that you make money in the collection.

Write down and quantify the bona fide environmental benefits of your product or process. One company was making plastic bags with 60 percent recycled content. This sounds great except it was using a 3-mil core of 100 percent recycled material with a 1-mil film of 100 percent virgin resin on each side (2 mils total). The result was a trash bag that was not as strong as a 1-mil-thick bag made from virgin material yet had twice the virgin plastic content. The core of the three-layer sandwich just became a place to throw out used plastic.

Ask, "What do people throw out that is not utilized? How can I secure a consistent supply of this material in a cost-effective, sustainable manner?"

If you make an existing product, make a list of the ten top raw materials you use. Where do you get the materials? Where do your suppliers get them? What are the steps employed to make them into the form you buy it in? Can any of the materials be sourced from materials someone discards? If you don't use raw materials but use value-added materials, think about what it would entail to produce one or more of those value-added materials yourself. For some companies that extrude mold plastic resin, it may merely take installing a grinder and a cleaning line.

Make a list of the top ten things your top ten customers throw out. Look at your own waste as a source of raw material. For example, Jody Wright's Motherwear used fabric scraps from its clothing to fill its nursing pillows. Reward employees for coming up with clever ideas on material sourcing. Think about the companies that replaced manufactured Styrofoam packaging inserts with shredded paper from their own office waste or die-cut corrugated paper made from boxes they received raw materials in. How about buying a shredder for your office and using the shredded paper for packing?

Summary

Turning waste into cash is not just good environmental stewardship, it's good business. Model sustainable businesses are collecting plastic lids to make toothbrushes, used shrink-wrap to make plastic buckets, discarded seat cushions to make tongues on shoes, human and animal excrement and garbage to create energy, soda bottles to make pet blankets, discarded building supplies to make furniture, and used vegetable oil to power vehicles and heat buildings. An abundant number of ways exist to turn trash into money. Here are just some of the steps you can take:

- List the raw materials you use and determine if these materials can be sourced from materials someone discards.
- List the things you and your customers throw away and determine if you can use any of these in your production.

- Source waste you can get consistently, in quantity, and in pure form and think of what you can make out of it.

- List materials that companies pay to throw away, get paid for removing them, and use them for a feedstock or fuelstock or get environmental credits for receiving them.

Afterword

Thank you for reading this book. We hope you found it helpful. Pursuing a sustainable enterprise is a noble endeavor. You will not be traveling in the footsteps of the status quo; you will be leading on a new path. The journey may be difficult and challenging, but ultimately, you will be creating a better quality of life for the next generation, and hopefully generations to come will recognize your sacrifices and effort.

We wrote this handbook on sustainability with the idea that it would cover the bulk—80 percent—of what it takes to be sustainable profitably. The truth is, now that you have begun to take the steps to achieve this 80 percent, you have probably found that you and your employees really like it. It's fun, it's a great outlet for your creativity, and it helps build camaraderie within the organization. You are "doing good, having fun, and making money."

You and your employees probably like it so much that you are coming up with your own creative thoughts, ideas, recommendations, and programs to become more sustainable profitably. That's what we meant by "Greening Your Organization's DNA" in the title.

DNA is a biological code that repeats itself on and on and on as long as there is life. If we were successful, your organization now has "green genes" and will work to make the sustainable choice going forward. We are completely confident that you and your employees know your business and what will be possible for it in terms of sustainable practices. Good luck. And if you have any challenges in going forward, contact us. We are always available to help and would love you to regale us with what you've done so far, what "ahas" you've experienced, and what "oh nos!" you've had along the way.

David Mager, DavidMager@comcast.net

Joe Sibila, joe@csrwire.com

www.streetsmartsustainability.com

Notes and Resources

Introduction

1. Natural Products Insider, "Nielsen Integrating NMI's LOHAS Model," February 26, 2008, http://www.naturalproducts insider.com/news/2008/02/nielsen-integrating-nmis-lohas -model.aspx.
2. Grocery Manufacturers Association and Deloitte, *Finding the Green in Today's Shoppers: Sustainability Trends and New Shopper Insights*, 2009, www.gmabrands.com/publications/ greenshopper09.pdf.
3. John Hechinger and Joseph Pereira, "Socially Conscious Investors Fear Ben & Jerry's Could Lose Its Flavor," *Wall Street Journal*, February 4, 2000.
4. Gasoline Alley Foundation, http://www.gasolinealleyfoun dation.org.
5. Green Seal, "82 Percent of Consumers Buying Green Despite Battered Economy," 2009, www.greenseal.org/resources/green_ buying_research.cfm.
6. Lifestyles of Health and Sustainability Online, "LOHAS Background," http://www.lohas.com/about.html.
7. David B. Montgomery and Catherine A. Ramus, "Corporate Social Responsibility Reputation Effects on MBA Job Choice" (research paper 1805, Graduate School of Business, Stanford University, 2003).
8. Net Impact, http://www.netimpact.org.
9. Office of Management and Budget, "Memorandum for Heads of Executive Departments and Agencies: Federal Participation in the Development and Use of Voluntary Consensus Standards and in Conformity Assessment Activities," Circular No. A-119, rev. February 10, 1998, http://www.whitehouse .gov/omb/rewrite/circulars/a119/a119.html.
10. Social Investment Forum Foundation, "2007 Report on Socially Responsible Investing Trends in the United States," 2007, http://www.socialinvest.org/resources/pubs/.

11. Investors' Circle, http://www.investorscircle.net.
12. United Nations Environment Programme Finance Initiative, "Demystifying Responsible Investment Performance," October 2007, http://www.unepfi.org/fileadmin/documents/ Demystifying_Responsible_Investment_Performance_01.pdf.
13. Sristudies.org, "Key Studies," http://www.sristudies.org/ Key+Studies, and "Bibliography," http://www.sristudies.org/ Bibliography.
14. KLD Indexes, "KLD Reports December 2008 Index Returns," press release, January 8, 2009, http://www.kld.com/newsletter/ archive/press/pdf/200901_Index_Performance.pdf.
15. Trish Hall, "How Youths Rallied to Dolphins' Cause," *New York Times,* April 18, 1990, www.nytimes.com/1990/04/ 18/garden/how-youths-rallied-to-dolphins-cause.html?page wanted=all.
16. Matthew L. Wald, "Earth Day at 20: How Green the Globe? A Special Report: Guarding Environment—A World of Challenges," *New York Times*, April 22, 1990.

Chapter 1

1. Gary Hirshberg, interview by David, November 5, 2009.
2. Horst Rechelbacher, interview by David, October 21, 2009.
3. Paulette Mae Cole, interview by David, November 10, 2009.
4. Greg Steltonpohl, interview by Joe, December 5, 2009.
5. Ibid.
6. Gary Hirshberg, interview by David, November 5, 2009.
7. Horst Rechelbacher, interview by David, October 21, 2009.
8. Brent Baker, interview by David, November 10, 2009.
9. Greg Steltonpohl, interview by Joe, December 5, 2009.
10. Abraham Maslow, "A Theory of Human Motivation," *Psychological Review* 50, no. 4 (1943): 370–396.

Chapter 2

1. SurveyMonkey, http://www.surveymonkey.com.
2. Zoomerang, http://www.zoomerang.com.
3. Federal Trade Commission, Bureau of Consumer Protection, "Guides for the Use of Environmental Marketing Claims," www.ftc.gov/bcp/grnrule/guides980427.htm.
4. F. J. Roethlisberger and William J. Dickson, *Management and the Worker: An Account of a Research Program Conducted by*

the Western Electric Company, Hawthorne Works, Chicago (Cambridge, MA: Harvard University Press, 1939).

5. Horst Rechelbacher, interview by David, October 21, 2009.

6. The following states have privilege or immunity laws or self-disclosure policies (U.S. Environmental Protection Agency, Region 5 Enforcement and Compliance, "State Audit Privilege and Immunity Laws & Self-Disclosure Laws and Policies," http://www.epa.gov/region5/enforcement/audit/stateaudit.html):

Alaska	Maine	Oklahoma
Arizona	Maryland	Oregon
Arkansas	Massachusetts	Pennsylvania
California	Michigan	Rhode Island
Colorado	Minnesota	South Carolina
Connecticut	Mississippi	South Dakota
Delaware	Montana	Tennessee
Florida	Nebraska	Texas
Hawaii	Nevada	Utah
Idaho	New Hampshire	Vermont
Illinois	New Jersey	Virginia
Indiana	New Mexico	Washington
Iowa	New York	Wisconsin
Kansas	North Carolina	
Kentucky	Ohio	

Chapter 3

1. Gary Hirshberg, interview by David, November 5, 2009.

2. Blag.biz, "Buddhism for Business," Bliss & Growth, http://blag.biz/buddhism-for-business.

3. International Organization for Standardization, http://www.iso.org.

4. Ontario Centre for Environmental Technology Advancement, "Environmental Management System Software," http://www.oceta.on.ca/profiles/greenware/greenwr.htm.

5. Environment International Limited, "Q & A: Environmental Management Systems and ISO 14000," http://www.eiltd.net/services/isoqa.shtml.

6. International Institute for Sustainable Development, *Global Green Standards: ISO 14000 and Sustainable Development* (Winnipeg, Manitoba: International Institute for Sustainable Development, 1996), http://www.iisd.org/pdf/globlgrn.pdf.

7. CERES, "CERES Principles," http://www.ceres.org/Page.aspx?pid=416.
8. Mindy Lubber, interview by David, April 6, 2010.
9. CERES. "The 21st Century Corporation: The CERES Roadmap for Sustainability," http://www.ceres.org/Page.aspx?pid=1211.
10. Horst Rechelbacher, interview by David, October 21, 2009.
11. Ibid.
12. Gary Hirshberg, interview by David, November 5, 2009.
13. The Natural Step, http://www.naturalstep.org.
14. The Natural Step, "Principles of Sustainability," http://www.naturalstep.org.
15. Global Reporting Initiative, http://www.globalreporting.org.
16. U.S. Environmental Protection Agency, "Materials Management & Human Health: Assessments & Performance Measures," http://www.epa.gov/sustainability/materials_assessments.htm.
17. Social Venture Network. "Standards of Corporate Social Responsibility." 1999, http://www.svn.org/_data/global/images/campaigns/CSR_standards.pdf.
18. Green Seal, http://www.greenseal.org.

Chapter 4

1. Horst Rechelbacher, interview by David, October 21, 2009.
2. Ibid.
3. William McDonough and Michael Braungart, *Cradle to Cradle: Remaking the Way We Make Things* (New York: North Point Press, 2002).
4. Gary Hirshberg, interview by David, November 5, 2009.
5. Horst Rechelbacher, interview by David, October 21, 2009.
6. Jody Wright, interview by David, October 27, 2009.
7. Wal-Mart Stores, Inc., "Sustainability Index," http://walmartstores.com/Sustainability/9292.aspx.
8. Sustainability Consortium, http://www.sustainabilityconsortium.org/.
9. The Life Cycle Initiative, http://www.estis.net/sites/lcinit/.
10. U.S. Environmental Protection Agency, "Life Cycle Assessment," http://www.epa.gov/nrmrl/lcaccess/index.html.
11. National Renewable Energy Laboratory "U.S. Life-Cycle Inventory Database," http://www.nrel.gov/lci.
12. See http://www.StreetSmartSustainability.com.

Chapter 5

1. Jef Sharp, interview by David, November 11, 2009.
2. Jeffrey Hollander, interview by Joe, December 5, 2009.
3. Following is a partial list of sustainability standard-setting organizations. (A list of other eco-labeling organizations is available at http://www.iatp.org/labels/envcommodities/eco-labels.html.)

   Blue Angel (Germany), http://www.blauer-engel.de/en/index.php—huge number of consumer, commercial, and building products and services; the first eco-labeling organization

   Eco-Logo, Environmental Choice (Canada), www.terrachoice-certified.com—consumer products

   Fair Trade Certified, www.transfairusa.org

   Green Seal (U.S.), www.greenseal.org—consumer products

   Indoor Environmental Standards Organization, www.iestandards.org

   International Standards Organization (ISO), http://www.iso.org

   Japan Environment Association (JEA), http://www.jeas.or.jp/ecomark/english/

   LEAF (Labeling Ecologically Approved Fabrics), www.LEAFCertified.org

   LEED—U.S. Green Building Council's Leadership in Energy and Environmental Design, http://www.usgbc.org/

   Nordic Countries Ecolabeling, http://www.ecolabel.nu/nordic_eco2/welcome/

   NSF International (National Sanitation Foundation), http://www.nsf.org—food, water, dietary supplements, sustainability

   Social Accountability International, www.sa-intl.org/—SA8000, global social accountability standard

4. Californians Against Waste, "Extended Producer Responsibility: A Legislative Model," http://www.cawrecycles.org/issues/epr.
5. Der Grüne Punkt, http://www.gruener-punkt.de/?L=1.
6. William McDonough Architects. "The Hannover Principles: Design for Sustainability," 1992, http://www.mcdonough.com/principles.pdf. One other source for green design insights is the following report: U.S. Congress, Office of Technology

Assessment, *Green Products by Design: Choices for a Cleaner Environment* (Washington, DC: U.S. Government Printing Office, 1992), www.fas.org/ota/reports/9221.pdf.

Chapter 6

1. Forest Stewardship Council, http://www.fscus.org.
2. Old Growth Again, http://www.foreverredwood.com.
3. Bamboo Sun, http://www.bamboosun.com.
4. Solar Living Institute, http://www.solarliving.org.
5. Real Goods, http://www.realgoods.com.
6. Laury Hammel, interview by David, November 4, 2009.
7. Tom Silverman, interview by David, November 19, 2009.
8. Paulette Mae Cole, interview by David, November 10, 2009.
9. Arcosanti, http://www.arcosanti.org.
10. Tom Horton, interview by David, November 6, 2009.
11. Ibid.
12. U.S. Green Building Council, www.usgbc.org.
13. Audubon International, http://www.auduboninternational.org.
14. Institute for Building Biology, http://www.buildingbiology.net.

Chapter 7

1. Everything on earth is powered by sunlight except nuclear, tidal, and geothermal power and the rotation of the earth.
2. To switch to a renewable energy source for the electricity you buy, contact National Grid, www.nationalgridus.com.
3. U.S. Environmental Protection Agency, "Green Power Partnership: Partner List," http://www.epa.gov/greenpower/partners/index.htm.
4. DSIRE: Database of State Incentives for Renewables and Efficiency, http://www.dsireusa.org.
5. U.S. Energy Information Administration, "Electricity Generation," http://www.eia.doe.gov/neic/infosheets/electric generation.html.
6. Jeffrey Logan and Stan Mark Kaplan, Congressional Research Service, *Wind Power in the United States: Technology, Economic, and Policy Issues,* June 20, 2008, www.fas.org/sgp/crs/misc/RL34546.pdf.
7. Aeronautica Windpower, http://www.aeronauticawind.com.
8. Solar Buzz. "Solar Electricity Global Price Benchmark Indices," June 2010, www.solarbuzz.com/solarindices.htm.

9. Steibel Eltron, "Sol 25 Plus Flat Plate Collector Technical Data," http://www.stiebel-eltron-usa.com/techdata_sol25.html.

10. Acorn Energy Coop, http://www.acornenergycoop.com.

11. Co-op Power, http://www.cooppower.coop.

12. Lynn Benander, interview by David, April 23, 2010.

13. DSIRE, http://www.dsireusa.org.

14. Yellow Biodiesel, http://www.YellowBiodiesel.com.

15. Zak Zaidman, interview by Joe, December 3, 2009.

16. Gary Hirshberg, interview by David, November 5, 2009.

17. U.S. Department of Energy, "U.S. Geothermal Resource Map," http://www1.eere.energy.gov/geothermal/printable_versions/geomap.html.

18. Bourke Builders, http://www.bourkebuilders.net, installs geothermal heaters and builds and renovates homes for people with chemical sensitivities.

19. Stacy C. Davis, Susan W. Diegel, and Robert G. Boundy, *Transportation Energy Data Book: Edition 28*, 2009, table 2.12, http://cta.ornl.gov/data/tedb28/Edition28_Full_Doc.pdf (accessed April 16, 2010).

20. Ibid.

21. Ibid.

22. Laury Hammel, interview by David, November 4, 2009.

23. Energy Star, "Air Seal and Insulate with Energy Star." http://www.energystar.gov/index.cfm?c=home_sealing.hm_improvement_sealing.

24. Energy Star, www.energystar.gov.

25. Laury Hammel, interview by David, November 4, 2009.

26. Environmental Research Laboratory, http://ag.arizona.edu/azaqua/erlhome.html.

27. Mal Warwick, interview by David, November 5, 2009.

Chapter 8

1. NSF International and Trucost Plc, *Carbon Emissions—Measuring the Risks*, 2009, http://www.nsf.org/business/sustainability/SUS_NSF_Trucost_Report.pdf.

2. Climate Counts, http://www.ClimateCounts.org.

3. See, for example, Carbonfund.org, http://www.carbonfund.org, and the Carbon Neutral Company, http://www.carbonneutral.com.

4. Carbon Concierge, http://www.carbonconcierge.com.

5. SocialCarbon, http://www.socialcarbon.org.

6. RainTrust Foundation, http://www.raintrust.org.
7. Cantor Fitzgerald, http://www.cantorco2e.com.
8. Element Markets, http://www.elementmarkets.com.
9. Evolution Markets, http://www.evomarkets.com.
10. Approximately 12% solids x approximately 75% volatile solids (VS) x 0.25 m^3 biogas/kg VS x 50% methane = volume of methane (in liters); 22.4 liters/mole = 16 grams/mole methane, which has a CO_2 equivalent of 23 times that of CO_2.
11. U.S. Department of Agriculture, Natural Resources Conservation Service, *Quantifying the Change in Greenhouse Gas Emissions Due to Natural Resource Conservation Practice Application in Indiana*, February 2002, http://www.in.nrcs.usda.gov/pdf%20files/Indiana_Final_Report.pdf.
12. Kenneth R. Richards, Robert J. Moulton, and Richard A. Birdsey, "Costs of Creating Carbon Sinks in the U.S.," *Energy Conservation and Management* 34, no. 9–11 (September–November 1993): 905–912.
13. Chicago Climate Exchange, http://www.chicagoclimatex.com.
14. Robert Kunzig, "Shading the Earth," The Big Idea, *National Geographic*, July 15, 2009, http://ngm.nationalgeographic.com/big-idea/01/shading-earth.
15. Hashem Akbari, Surabi Menon, and Arthur Rosenfeld, "Global Cooling: Increasing World-wide Urban Albedos to Offset CO_2," *Climatic Change* 94, no. 3–4 (June 2009): 275–286, http://www.springerlink.com/content/r465853147015k4g/fulltext.pdf.

Chapter 9

1. Gary Hirshberg, interview by David, November 5, 2009.
2. Ibid.
3. Social(k), http://www.socialk.com.
4. Heather White, interview by David, August 21, 2009.
5. Verité, http://www.verite.org.
6. Dean Cycon, interview by David, July 6, 2009.
7. Joseph Whinney and Andy McShea, interview by David and facility tour, July 1, 2009.
8. Wal-Mart Stores, Inc., "Walmart Announces Sustainable Product Index," CSRwire, July 16, 2009, http://www.csrwire.com/press/press_release/27347-Walmart-Announces-Sustainable-Product-Index.
9. Paulette Mae Cole, interview by David, November 10, 2009.

10. Evo, http://www.evostore.info.

11. Evo, "Defining the Total Environmental Impact: Part 1," http://evostore.info/content/2924/defining_the_total_environ mental_impact_-_part_1.

12. Association of California Water Agencies and California Department of Water Resources, "Save Our Water," in "Water: Our Thirsty World," special issue, *National Geographic* (April 2010).

13. Horst Rechelbacher, interview by David, October 21, 2009.

14. Alan D. Dangour et al., "Nutrition-Related Health Effects of Organic Foods: A Systematic Review," *American Journal of Clinical Nutrition* 92, no. 1 (2010) doi:10.3945/ajcn.2010.29269.

15. Betty K. Ishida and Mary H. Chapman, "A Comparison of Carotenoid Content and Total Antioxidant Activity in Catsup from Several Commercial Sources in the United States," *Journal of Agricultural and Food Chemistry* 52, no. 26 (2004), doi:10.1021/jf040154o.

16. Environmental Working Group, "EWG Updates the Pesticide Shopper's Guide," EWG.org, March 10, 2009, http://www.ewg.org/newsrelease/EWG-New-Pesticide-Shoppers-Guide.

17. U.S. Department of Agriculture, "National Organic Program," http://www.ams.usda.gov/nop.

18. See, for example, Institute for Local Self-Reliance, "The Economic Impact of Locally Owned Businesses vs. Chains: A Case Study in Midcoast Maine," September 2003, http://www.newrules.org/sites/newrules.org/files/midcoaststudy.pdf.

19. Business Alliance for Local Living Economies, http://www.livingeconomies.org.

20. Community Involved in Sustainable Agriculture, http://www.buylocalfood.com.

21. Local Harvest, http://www.localharvest.org/csa/.

22. Lancaster Farm Fresh Cooperative, http://www.lancasterfarm fresh.com.

23. Bon Appétit Management Company, "Bon Appétit Management Company Proves Buying Local Food Is Scalable for Business with Landmark of $55mm in Purchases," CSRwire, February 6, 2007, http://www.csrwire.com/press _releases/19373-Bon-App-tit-Management-Company-Proves-Buying-Local-Food-is-Scalable-for-Business-with-Land mark-of-55mm-in-Purchases.

24. Judy Wicks, interview by Joe, December 2, 2009.
25. Western States Contracting Alliance, http://www.aboutwsca.org.
26. International Green Purchasing Network, http://www.igpn.org.
27. Green America, http://www.greenamericatoday.org.

Chapter 10

1. Zero Emissions Research and Initiatives, http://www.zeri.org.
2. Green Festival, http://www.greenfestivals.org.
3. John P. Chastain, "Pollution Potential of Livestock Manure," *Minnesota/Wisconsin Engineering Notes* (Winter 1995), http://www.bbe.umn.edu/extens/ennotes/enwin95/manure.html.
4. The Pennsylvania State University, Crop Management Extension Group, The Penn State Agronomy Guide (2010) table 1.2-14, http://agguide.agronomy.psu.edu/cm/pdf/table1-2-14.pdf.
5. Gary Hirshberg, interview by David, November 5, 2009.
6. Josh Goldman, interview by Joe, November 23, 2009.
7. "Standards for the Use or Disposal of Sewage Sludge," Code of Federal Regulations, title 40, part 503, e-CFR, http://ecfr.gpoaccess.gov/cgi/t/text/text-idx?c=ecfr&tpl=/ecfrbrowse/Title40/40cfr503_main_02.tpl (accessed June 22, 2010).
8. Pennsylvania General Assembly, Legislative Budget and Finance Committee, *Chesapeake Bay Tributary Strategy Compliance Cost Study* (Harrisburg, PA: 2008), www.lbfc.legis.state.pa.us/reports/2008/25.PDF.
9. Red Barn Trading Company, http://www.redbarntrading.com.
10. Universal Remediation Inc., http://www.unireminc.com.
11. U.S. Environmental Protection Agency, Toxics Release Inventory Program, "EPCRA Section 313 Chemical List for Reporting Year 2006 (Including Toxic Chemical Categories)," 2006, http://www.epa.gov/tri/trichemicals/chemicallists/RY2006ChemicalList.pdf.
12. TerraCycle, "TerraCycle Plant Food Becomes First Consumer Product to Earn Zerofootprint Seal," CSRwire, August 22, 2006, http://www.csrwire.com/press/press_release/17577-TerraCycle-Plant-Food-153-Becomes-First-Consumer-Product-to-Earn-Zerofootprint-153-Seal.
13. Springfield Materials Recycling Facility, http://springfieldmrf.org.

14. Meredith Corporation, "2007 Top 25 Green Cities in America," *Country Home*, 2007, http://www.countryhome.com/greencities/top25_2007.html.

15. Greenopolis, "Waste Management Partner Sustainability Plan." http://greenopolis.com/partners/wm-partner/sustainability_plan.

16. Silicon Valley Toxic Corporation, "Poison PCs/Toxic TVs," 2004, http://www.svtc.org/site/DocServer/ppcttv2004.pdf?docID=301.

17. U.S. Environmental Protection Agency, Wastes Department, "Fact Sheet: Management of Electronic Waste in the United States," April 2007 (revised July 2008), http://www.epa.gov/waste/conserve/materials/ecycling/docs/fact7-08.pdf.

18. U.S. Environmental Protection Agency, Wastes Department, "Plug-in to eCycling," www.epa.gov/epawaste/partnerships/plugin/index.htm.

Chapter 11

1. Donald L. Klass, *Biomass for Renewable Energy, Fuels and Chemicals* (San Diego: Academic Press, 1998).

2. Julie Lewis, interview by David, June 18, 2009.

3. Bion Environmental Technologies, http://www.biontech.com.

4. Worldwise, http://www.worldwise.com.

Resource A

Cover Letter and Employee Questionnaire

This sample cover letter and questionnaire are available on our Web site, www.streetsmartsustainability.com, translated into many languages. If you speak a language for which we don't have a translation, please translate these items for us and we will post them on our Web site and acknowledge your input.

Dear Valued Employee:

Our concern for sustainability, the environment, and social responsibility is one of the highest priorities of this company. As another step in making continuous improvement toward excellent sustainable practices, we are about to have a comprehensive sustainability audit performed.

A key part of the sustainability audit will be a confidential survey of the employees. You can respond to the survey questionnaire online or by mail. You have the option to fill out the questionnaire anonymously. What is important to us is to learn what you feel are the company's strengths and weaknesses in fulfilling its environmental and socially responsible commitments and what you feel are steps we could take to improve this company.

Please take a few minutes to answer the form completely and honestly by ___ (day of week, date). Use extra paper if you need to expand on your answers.

Thank you,

Signed by _____

Boss / President / CEO / Owner / Executive Director

Employee Questionnaire

Question 1: How many miles do you live from work? How do you commute (car, car/van pool, public transportation, motorcycle, bicycle, walking)?

Question 2: Do you know the company's environmental and sustainability policies?

Question 3: Have you provided management with ideas to improve the company's environmental and sustainability performance (energy conservation, waste reduction, purchasing, etc.)?

Question 4: Have any of these ideas been implemented?

Question 5: Does management encourage employees to be environmentally and socially responsible *within the company*?

Question 6: Does management encourage employees to be environmentally and socially responsible *outside the company*?

Question 7: Which statement best describes management's position on the environment and social responsibility?

   a. Concern for the environment and social responsibility are among the company's highest goals, and the company continuously works to make improvements.
   b. The company does much to ensure that it is environmentally and socially responsible.

c. The company does whatever it can to be environmentally and socially responsible, providing that it is cost-effective.

d. The company only does what it is required by law to do. Concern for the environment and social responsibility are not high on the company's list of priorities.

e. Management would knowingly violate environmental, safety, human rights, and/or other laws if they thought they could get away with it.

Question 8: What is the company's number one environmental strength?

Question 9: What is the company's number one environmental weakness?

Question 10: What is your top recommendation for making the company as a whole more environmentally responsible?

Question 11: What is your top recommendation for making your department more environmentally responsible?

Provide additional space for the employee to voluntarily put his or her job title and name; some employees may and some may not offer this information.

Resource B

Audit Protocol

What follows is a protocol for performing your sustainability audit.

I. Policy
    A. Do you have a sustainability policy statement?
    B. Has it been approved by senior management?
    C. Is it in the employee handbook? And visible to customers? Vendors? Stockholders? Other stakeholders (e.g., the community)?

II. Sustainability Aspects
    A. Does the enterprise have a procedure to determine the company's key aspects and impacts on sustainability? (See chapter 4 on metrics.)
    B. Does the sustainability policy address these issues?

III. Legal and Other Requirements
    A. Does the company have a procedure for knowing what federal, state, and local laws it must comply with?
    B. Is the company in compliance with those laws?
    C. Has the company voluntarily committed to comply with any other rules or principles (CERES, Natural Step, Trade Association of Ethical Standards, living wage, fair trade, organic, etc.)?
    D. Is the company in compliance with these other rules it volunteered to comply with?

IV. Environmental Management System
   A. Does the company have an environmental management system (EMS) or environmental contract?
   B. Does it set objectives and goals for each of the areas the company is targeting with performance dates?
   C. Is there a code of ethical conduct for senior management?
   D. Does the EMS delineate responsible personnel and specify to whom they report?
   E. Is there a procedure for training employees in their responsibilities regarding the company's sustainability plans, for checking their compliance and competence, and for rewarding their performance?
   F. Is the EMS well documented? And is there a procedure for documentation revision and for removing out-of-date documentation?
   G. Has the organization assigned sufficient management, employees, and other resources to implement the EMS?
   H. Is there a procedure for dealing with nonconformance with the EMS, for making corrections, and for preventing nonconformance?
   I. Is there a procedure for anticipating, preventing, and dealing with emergencies, including regulated emergencies (oil spill), natural disasters (fire, flood, and swine flu outbreak), or business emergencies (interruption of incoming supply, brownout, etc.)
   J. Is there a procedure for communicating the results of this audit internally and externally?

K. Does the EMS adequately deal with monitoring and measurement of EMS parameters and keeping EMS records? (For more details, see chapter 4.)

V. Environmental Attributes

A. Energy Use and Conservation—Details on calculating energy use are covered in chapter 7.

B. Water Use and Conservation—How much water do you use in total? For incorporation into products? For buildings? For grounds? For manufacturing? For heating and cooling? How much gray water do you use?

C. Material Use and Conservation—Make a manifest and quantify all the items you buy, inventory, and use. If the task seems daunting, make a list of the top ten items you buy, inventory, and use. Include the number of units and the weight and volume of each unit. A more detailed assessment called an input/output mass balance analysis is covered in chapter 4.

D. Releases to Water—How much sewage does your business produce per year? Do you pay for metered sewage services, and if so, what is your total suspended solids (TSS), biological oxygen demand (BOD), chemical oxygen demand (COD), total oxygen demand (TOD), grease/oil, and total Kjehdahl nitrogen (TKN) per year? Is any on-site water treatment conducted? Quantify its impact on releases. The Toxic Release Inventory (TRI) requires that companies that produce over a certain amount of toxic waste report what their releases to water and emissions to air are. Quantify your releases to water of each compound you use and dispose of. List the amount of nutrient or sediment credits you purchase (or produce); it is worth knowing that the mandatory reporting of releases of toxic chemicals is the single greatest factor in their reduced use.

E. Emissions to Air—Quantify your releases to air of regulated and nonregulated substances. Your emissions to air of carbon dioxide are examined in chapter 8. Quantify how many environmental credits (VOCs, NO_x, SO_x, etc.) you use or produce.

F. Solids—What is the weight of material you reuse each year? What is the weight of material you recycle each year? What is the weight of material you dispose of each year? What is your percent diversion (weight of material used and recycled divided by weight of material used, recycled, and thrown out). Use a random number generator to pick a day and container on which to do a "dump dive" and quantify what is in your waste.

Resource C

Summary of ISO 14001— Environmental Management Systems

What follows are the section names and descriptions of the criteria within the global standards for environmental management systems.

1. Environmental Policy—Develop a policy statement of the organization's commitment to the environment.
2. Environmental Aspects and Impacts—Identify the environmental aspects of products, activities, and services and their effects on the environment.
3. Legal and Other Requirements—Identify and ensure compliance with pertinent laws and regulations.
4. Objectives and Targets and Environmental Management Program—Set environmental goals for the enterprise and plan actions to achieve the objectives and targets.
5. Structure and Responsibility—Assign environmental roles and responsibilities within the organization.
6. Training, Awareness, and Competence—Make sure that employees are aware and capable of carrying out their environmental responsibilities.
7. Communication—Develop processes for internally and externally communicating environmental management issues.
8. EMS Documentation—Maintain information about the environmental management system and related documents.

9. Document Control—Ensure that everyone who should has the current EMS and related documents and that no one has outdated documents.

10. Operational Control—Identify, plan, and manage the organization's operations and activities in a manner that is consistent with the policy, objectives and targets, and significant aspects of the EMS.

11. Emergency Preparedness and Response—Develop procedures for preventing potential emergencies and responding to real emergencies.

12. Monitoring and Measuring—Periodically monitor and measure major activities and track compliance.

13. Evaluation of Compliance—Develop procedures to periodically determine compliance with legal and other requirements.

14. Nonconformance and Corrective and Preventive Action—Identify and correct problems and prevent them from recurring.

15. Records—Adequately record performance of the EMS.

16. EMS Audit—Periodically verify that the EMS is effective in achieving the objectives and targets.

17. Management Review—Review, revise, and improve the EMS.

Resource D

Input/Output Mass Balance Analysis

As part of the input/output mass balance analysis (IOMBA), quantify each of the following input and output items:

Input

Weight of incoming freight, including the weight of packaging

Weight of incoming mail and packages

Weight of incoming office supplies

Weight of incoming water

Weight of items brought in by employees, customers, and visitors that are left on-site

Output

Weight of mail and product shipped to or carried off by customers, including the weight of packaging

Weight of water leaving the facility

Weight of material leaving the facility for recycling

Weight of material leaving the facility for composting

Weight of material going to a proprietary wastewater treatment facility

Weight of material leaving the facility for disposal, including the weight of material leaving the company's own wastewater treatment facility for disposal

Weight of total suspended solids (TSS), biological
   oxygen demand (BOD), chemical oxygen demand
   (COD), and/or total oxygen demand (TOD) disposed
   of via the sewer to a municipal wastewater treatment
   facility
Weight of grease and oil disposed of via the sewer to a
   municipal wastewater treatment facility
Weight of material leaving the facility through the
   smokestack
Weight of all other emissions, e.g., concentration of
   volatile organic compounds in the facility's air times
   the fresh air exchange rate

Sample IOMBA for Milk as a Raw Material

Whole milk is 100 percent of your ingredients. Analysis
of the total grease and oil in your sewage is 100 milligrams
per liter. With a water discharge rate of 5,000 gallons per day,
at 3.75 liters per gallon and 250 days of production per year,
468,750,000 milligrams of fat is discharged into the sewage
per year.

This 468,750,000 milligrams of fat divided by 453,592
milligrams per pound equals 1,033 pounds of fat discharged
into the sewage per year.

Whole milk is 3.5 percent fat content and has a density of
8.6 pounds per gallon. To convert the milk fat into gallons of
milk lost, divide 1,033 pounds by 3.5 percent (0.035) to get
29,514 pounds of milk discharged down the sewer each year.

When you then divide 29,514 pounds by 8.6 pounds per
gallon, you'll find out that you are losing 3,432 gallons of
whole milk down the drain per year.

Resource E

Life Cycle Analysis Matrix

The following instructions and table provide the basis for you to determine the impact of your products or services in every stage of their life cycle as explained in chapter 4.

Instructions—In each box (for example, the box that intersects Energy and Distribution), write the quantity used in association with this aspect of the product's or service's life cycle (in this case, gallons or Btu of fuel used per year) or write its quality (e.g., major energy use). After the boxes are filled in, use a red, yellow, or green highlighter to color each box: red for major impact, yellow for minor impact, and green for no impact. This will make it easier to see where the significant life cycle impacts are for your products, processes, or services. Every blank box represents an area where you have a blind spot about your product's impact on the environment. As you learn more about your product over time, update the matrix.

Product/ Service Name	Preproduction	Manufacturing	Packaging	Distribution	Use	Disposal
Inputs Energy						
Water						
Material						
Outputs Emissions to air*						
Releases to water†						
Solid waste						
Ecological considerations						
Toxicological considerations						

* Emissions to air including greenhouse warming, acidification, ozone layer destroying, eutrophication, and photochemical reactions
† Releases to water including impact on eutrophication and acidification

EXAMPLE
Major impact = bold
Minor impact = *italics*

Product name: MILK	Preproduction	Manufacturing	Packaging	Distribution	Use	Disposal
Inputs						
Energy	**Cleaning cows and equipment, cooling milk**	*Pasteurizing then cooling*		*Refrigerated trucking and Refrigerated cases*		
Water	**100+ gal per cow/day**	*to wash equipment*				
Material			*HDPE[3] or PE[4] coated paper cartons*			
Outputs						
Emissions to air[1]	**Methane— GWG[1] ammonia**, *VOCs[2]—ozone, odor*	CO_2 – GWG[1]		CO_2 – GWG[1], NO_x Hydrocarbons PM[3]		

Releases to water[2]	Nitrogen and Phosphorus—eutrophication	Detergent to wash equipment		BOD[6] Nitrogen and Phosphorus, Grease/Fat
Solid waste				99% cartons and 81% HDPE[3] bottles go to landfill
Ecological considerations				
Toxicological considerations	E. coli, pathogens	Dioxins in paper		

* Emissions to air including greenhouse warming, acidification, ozone layer destroying, eutrophication, and photochemical reactions

† Releases to water including impact on eutrophication and acidification

[1] GWG—Greenhouse warming gas

[2] VOCs—Volatile organic compounds

[3] HDPE—High-Density polyethylene

[4] PE—Polyethylene

[5] PM—Particulate matter

[6] BOD—Biological oxygen demand

Resource F

Energy Source Calculator

By reviewing your monthly energy bills for the previous twelve months you can quantify your energy use by converting different kinds of energy or fuel into one standard measure—million Btu. In this way, you can compare energy sources and make informed decisions. For more information, see chapter 7.

Fuel[1]	Unit	Energy/Unit	Energy Unit	Million Btu/Unit
Oil	gallon	0.13	million Btu	0.1381
Gasoline	gallon	115,000	Btu	0.1150
Petrodiesel	gallon	130,500	Btu	0.1305
Natural gas HHV	100 ft[3]	102,700	Btu	0.1027
Natural gas LHV	100 ft[3]	93,000	Btu	0.0930
Natural gas	therm	1.00	100,000 Btu	0.1000
Propane[2]	gallon	91,547	Btu	0.0915
Propane[2]	pound	21,591	Btu	0.0216
Coal (bituminous/anthracite)	metric tonne	25.67	million Btu	25.6721
Coal (lignite/subbituminous)	metric tonne	14.26	million Btu	14.2623
Coal (bituminous/anthracite)	U.S. ton	23.29	million Btu	23.2959
Coal (lignite/subbituminous)	U.S. ton	12.94	million Btu	12.9422
Wood (bone dry)	cord	18.24	million Btu	18.2400
Wood (air dried—20% moisture content)	cord	15.36	million Btu	15.3600
Charcoal	pound	12,800	Btu	0.0128
Ethanol	gallon	75,700	Btu	0.0757
Biodiesel	gallon	118,734	Btu	0.1187
Electricity[3] from coal	kWh	1.00	kWh	0.0034
Electricity[3] from petroleum	kWh	1.00	kWh	0.0034
Electricity[3] from gas	kWh	1.00	kWh	0.0034
U.S. average electricity	kWh	1.00	kWh	0.0034

[1] http://bioenergy.ornl.gov/papers/misc/energy_convhtml
[2] www.eia.doe.gov/cneaf/electricity/page/co2_reportco2emiss.pdf
[3] www.epa.gov/OMS/climate/420f05001.htm

Resource G

Carbon Footprint Calculator

To calculate your total carbon footprint, take the numbers from your energy audit in chapter 7 and put them in column A below. Multiply each item in column A by the corresponding number in column B. Then divide by 2,000 to calculate the number of tons of CO_2 for each energy source. Add up all the numbers in the last column to calculate your total carbon footprint. For more information, see chapter 8.

Fuel	A. Million Btu per year	B. Pounds of CO_2/million Btu	(A x B) /2000 = tons of CO_2 per year
Oil/diesel		161	
Gasoline		156	
Natural gas		117	
Liquefied natural gas		139	
Propane		139	
Coal		205	
Electricity		131	
Your total carbon footprint from energy use of the above (add up all numbers in the last column)			

Example

Fuel	A. Million Btu per year	B. Pounds of CO_2/million Btu	(A x B) / 2000 = tons of CO_2 per year
Oil/diesel	10,000 gal oil = 1,380 MBtu and 25,000 gal diesel = 3,263 MBtu = 4,643 MBtu	161	747,523 pounds = 373.8 tons CO_2
Gasoline	2,500 gal = 288 MBtu	156	22.4
Natural gas		117	
Liquefied natural gas		139	
Propane		139	
Coal		205	
Electricity	175,320 kWh = 596 MBtu	131	39.0
Your total carbon footprint from energy use of the above (add up all numbers in the last column)			435.2 tons of CO_2 per year

Resource H

Vendor Questionnaire

What follows are general and specific questions to ask your vendors to qualify their environmental performance, which is subsidized by your purchasing dollars.

General Vendor Questions

1. What is the minimum wage paid to employees? What is the minimum wage paid to contract employees who work within your facilities (e.g., cleaning contractors)? What is the minimum wage paid at your top ten vendors? What is the ratio of your highest salary to your lowest salary for a full-time employee?
2. What is the ethnodemographic breakdown of your employees? Of management? As it relates to the U.S. Census data for the region? Do you provide specific training to HR personnel and managers in managing diversity?
3. What is the percentage diversion of waste produced in your facility?
4. What percent of employees do not walk to work or use bicycles, car/van pools, or public transportation to get to work?
5. Is the majority of lighting employed in the offices energy efficient? Is your office equipment Energy Star rated?
6. Please send us your mission statement and list your top socially and environmentally responsible sustainability practices.

7. What is the employee turnover rate? What is the average number of years of employment?
8. Do you incentivize employee social activism? Work-life balance? And if so, how?
9. If you produce an annual sustainability report, please send it or a link to it.

Plastic and Plastic Packaging Suppliers

1. Are the plastics you use for our products synthesized from renewable, natural ingredients (cotton, sawdust, etc.)? From natural gas? From petrochemicals?
2. Do the plastics produce volatiles or release gases during or after molding?
3. What are the percentages of nonusable waste material and recyclable scrap produced during molding?
4. Do you regrind and reuse your own scrap?
5. What are the dyes and fillers used in the plastic?
6. Are plasticizers used in the plastic? Are they made from natural ingredients (beef fat, soybean, or linseed oil) or synthetic ingredients (phosphate and phthalate)?
7. Do the plastics contain fire retardants? Are they halogenated? Are they listed on MSDS sheets?
8. What mold release chemicals are used, if any?
9. What inks and solvents are used in printing on the plastics? Are they free of lead, mercury, cadmium, and hexavalent chromium?
10. Is ink curing by thermal, UV, or radiation methods?
11. Have you had your containers tested for compliance with requirements for nontoxics in packaging?
12. What is the percentage, if any, of recycled material used in the manufacture of the plastic products we buy from you? What percentage is postconsumer recycled?

13. What plastic resins are used in the products we buy from you?
14. If the plastics are metallized, is this done with an electroless plating process or with vacuum metallization?

Fiberboard and Corrugated Box and Paper Bag Supplies

1. What is the percentage of recycled fiber and postconsumer waste in the boxes?
2. Is the fiber unbleached or bleached without chlorine?
3. Are you in compliance with voluntary requirements for reduction of toxics in packaging? If yes, what are your current measured levels of lead, mercury, cadmium, and hexavalent chromium?
4. Do you print with soy-based inks? If not, what is your percent solids?
5. Do you use inks, dyes, and pigments that meet the requirements of ASTM D-4236 for nontoxicity?
6. What is the percentage of scrap from die cutting the boxes? What is its disposition (is it recycled)?

Suppliers

1. For each of the top five chemicals you supply us, list the percentages of the principal ingredients (other than water) derived in whole from plants, derived in whole from plants using organic agricultural practices, synthesized from plant materials, synthesized from chemicals (petrochemicals), or mined and/or refined. Please list each chemical separately.
2. For chemicals sold in bulk in drums and/or buckets, do you have a program for taking back the drums and/or buckets and either refilling them or recycling them?

3. For any materials sold to us, did you have any reporting requirements under the Toxic Release Inventory (SARA Title III Sec 313) program? Please send copies of or links to the most recent publicly disclosed reports.

4. Are the chemicals sold to us biodegradable? What test method did you employ?

5. Are you a member, a signatory of, or in compliance with any of the following voluntary programs:

    Chemical Manufacturers Association Responsible CARE program?

    CERES Principles?

    Global Environmental Management Initiative (GEMI)?

    International Chamber of Commerce (ICC) Business Charter for Sustainable Development?

    International Standards Organization (ISO) ISO 14001 Standard for Environmental Management Systems?

    Other?

6. Do you have regular internal or third-party environmental audits for environmental regulatory compliance? For environmental management systems? Of regulated and nonregulated releases to air or water and solid and hazardous waste?

7. Do you participate in any of the EPA's voluntary Common Sense Pollution Prevention initiatives? Please list the programs you participated in for the current year.

8. Do you participate in any of the state or local government voluntary pollution prevention initiatives?

9. Do you prepare an annual environmental report available to shareholders and/or the public? Does it comply with the Public Environmental Reporting Initiative (PERI) Guidelines? Please include a copy of your most recent report.

Index

About Social Venture Network

SVN transforms the way the world does business by connecting, leveraging, and promoting a global community of leaders for a more just and sustainable economy.

Since its founding in 1987, SVN has grown from a handful of visionary individuals into a vibrant community of five hundred business owners, investors, and nonprofit leaders who are advancing the movement for social responsibility in business. SVN members believe in a new bottom line for business, one that values healthy communities and the human spirit as well as high returns.

As a network, SVN facilitates partnerships, strategic alliances, and other ventures that promote social and economic justice. SVN collects and promotes best practices for socially responsible enterprises and produces unique conferences that support the professional and personal development of business leaders and social entrepreneurs.

Please visit www.svn.org for more information on SVN membership, initiatives, and events.

About the Authors

David Mager

While attending Stuyvesant High School in New York in 1968, David Mager helped organize high schools in the United States and around the world for the first Earth Day. Since that time he has worked with over 300 companies, including General Electric, General Motors, IBM, Anheuser-Busch, Nestle, Coca-Cola, Hallmark, CitiGroup, Unilever, and Amoco, in helping them become greener profitably. A pioneer in performing comprehensive sustainability audits, David has worked with many socially responsible companies including Stonyfield Farm, Aveda, Gaiam, Tommy Boy Entertainment, and Rhino Records, Motherwear, Mal Warwick Associates, and Eileen Fisher.

David was fortunate to serve as an advisor on the Obama USDA Transition Team in helping prepare incoming Secretary Thomas Vilsack on the issues of sustainability, organics and farm-to-table, renewable energy, and the environmental footprint of agriculture. As director of standards of the first U.S. environmental certification and labeling organization, Green Seal, David oversaw the development of U.S. and global environmental standards for energy-efficient lighting, water-efficient fixtures, recycled paper, rerefined engine oil, household cleaners, paints, appliances, and other consumer products.

David represented the United States and the American National Standards Institute at the United Nations in the creation of the global ISO 14000 standards for environmental management systems. He also worked with the U.S. EPA in the creation of the life cycle analysis methodology.

David reuses, recycles, and composts; walks, runs, bikes, canoes, or drives a hybrid; washes his clothes in cold water and line drys them; and lives in a wood-heated, converted tobacco barn on the banks of the Connecticut River in the Pioneer Valley with Sadie Sunrise, the youngest of his three daughters and his wife, Deborah.

PHOTO BY JEFF FELDMAN

Joe Sibilia

As a visionary of the socially responsible business movement, Joe Sibilia is founder and CEO of Meadowbrook Lane Capital, described by the *Wall Street Journal* as a "socially responsible investment bank," specializing in turning values into valuation. Meadowbrook Lane is widely recognized for its work preserving the social and environmental initiatives of Ben & Jerry's and its work developing proprietary formulas and technology eliminating bottles and cans in food serving operations, which was ultimately purchased by the Pepsi-Cola Company. Meadowbrook Lane Capital has bought and sold nineteen companies at varying stages of sustainability development.

Joe is also CEO of CSRwire.com, a digital media property distributing, archiving, and innovating information that advances the corporate social responsibility movement toward a more economically just and environmentally sustainable society for professionals and affinity groups in over 200 countries. CSRwire.com has over 5,000 members worldwide.

Joe also founded the Gasoline Alley Foundation, a 501(c)3 nonprofit that has incubated forty-three small businesses and teaches inner-city and underprivileged persons to become successful entrepreneurs using socially responsible/sustainable business practices while revitalizing inner city neighborhoods. The foundation gives value to that which has been abandoned.

He serves on a number of boards, is a deputy sheriff of Hampden County, Massachusetts, and has been the longest serving board member of Social Venture Network.

Joe is the husband of Claire Sullivan, noted school psychologist, and father of three daughters: Kristen, Kendra, and Kayla. The Sibilia family lives in western Massachusetts with their dog Finally.

Other Titles in the Social Venture Network Series

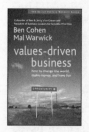

Values-Driven Business

How to Change the World, Make Money, and Have Fun

Ben Cohen and Mal Warwick

Ben & Jerry's cofounder Ben Cohen and Social Venture Network chair Mal Warwick team up to provide you with a complete guide to running your business for profit and personal satisfaction. This book details every step in the process of creating and managing a business that will reflect your personal values, not force you to hide them. It includes a self-assessment tool to determine what it will take to start a values-based business or transform your company into one, as well as scores of real-world examples and practical suggestions.

192 pages, ISBN 978-1-57675-358-3 • PDF ebook, ISBN 978-1-57675-951-6

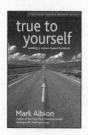

True to Yourself

Leading a Values-Based Business

Mark Albion

How do you build a company that serves people and the planet and turns a profit? What do you do when you believe that business should serve the common good, but everyday business pressures—meeting payroll, battling competition, keeping customers and investors happy—are at a fever pitch? The author of the *New York Times* bestseller *Making a Life, Making a Living* provides tools as well as advice from seventy-five forward-looking leaders to help you combine profit with purpose, margin with mission, value with values.

192 pages, ISBN 978-1-57675-378-1 • PDF ebook, ISBN 978-1-57675-950-9

Marketing That Matters

10 Practices to Profit Your Business and Change the World

Chip Conley and Eric Friedenwald-Fishman

Award-winning marketers Conley and Friedenwald-Fishman prove that marketing is key to advancing both the value and values of any business. They offer ten innovative marketing techniques—from discovering how customers make decisions to building committed communities of customers, employees, and strategic partners who will spread the word about your company—that will help you engage your customers and potentially change the world.

216 pages, ISBN 978-1-57675-383-5 • PDF ebook, ISBN 978-1-57675-964-6

Other Titles in the Social Venture Network Series

Growing Local Value
How to Build Business Partnerships That Strengthen Your Community
Laury Hammel and Gun Denhart

Turn your business into a good citizen and you can help ensure its success and contribute to making your community a great place to live and work. Hanna Andersson founder Gun Denhart and BALLE cofounder Laury Hammel show how you can leverage every aspect of your business—product creation to employee recruitment, vendor selection, capital raising, and more—to benefit both the community and the bottom line.

192 pages, ISBN 978-1-57675-371-2 • PDF ebook, ISBN 978-1-57675-960-8

Values Sell
Transforming Purpose into Profit Through Creative Sales and Distribution Strategies
Nadine A. Thompson and Angela E. Soper

Thompson and Soper draw on real-world examples to detail concrete steps for designing sales and distribution strategies that fit the needs, habits, and interests of your target customers. They show how to turn your stakeholders into enthusiastic partners by ensuring that all your relationships—with your salespeople, other employees, your customers, and your suppliers—are beneficial and fulfilling on more than just an economic level.

192 pages, ISBN 978-1-57675-421-4 • PDF ebook, ISBN 978-1-57675-520-4

Mission, Inc.
The Practitioner's Guide to Social Enterprise
Kevin Lynch and Julius Walls, Jr.

A new breed of business is springing up across the land: social enterprises, whose primary purpose is to support the common good. Lynch and Walls, Jr., explore ten key paradoxes of social enterprises and, using their own hard-won experiences and those of twenty other social enterprise leaders, show how to navigate the extreme challenges and seize the tremendous opportunities these organizations present.

216 pages, ISBN 978-1-57675-479-5 • PDF ebook, ISBN 978-1-57675-618-8

Dealing with the Tough Stuff
Practical Wisdom for Running a Values-Driven Business
Margot Fraser and Lisa Lorimer

When you're actually running a values-driven business, problems come up that you never could have anticipated. Birkenstock founder Margot Fraser and Lisa Lorimer are here to help. Together with five of their colleagues—including Stonyfield Farm founder Gary Hirshberg and former Ms. Foundation president Marie C. Wilson—they offer the kinds of personal insights and seasoned advice you just can't get in business school. It's like sitting down at the table with some of the nation's top socially conscious entrepreneurs.

240 pages, ISBN 978-1-57675-665-2 • PDF book, ISBN 978-1-57675-868-7

About This Book

This book is printed on Cascade's Rolland Enviro 100 paper, which is a 100 percent postconsumer-waste recycled paper. Compared to a virgin paper of the same weight, one ton of paper (the equivalent of approximately 3,080 books) saves the following resources:

26 trees

15,696 gallons of water

1,663 pounds of solid waste

4 tons of carbon dioxide emissions

the energy equivalent of 331 gallons of oil

The paper manufacturing facility is powered entirely by renewable energy hydropower and biogas.

The above is based upon an analysis conducted by Climate forIdeas.org using data from a report prepared for Cascade by Dessau Engineering and Construction and the Environmental Defense Fund's Paper Task Force initiative and paper calculator.

The printer, Malloy Inc., is a family-owned book printer that uses both Forest Stewardship Council and Sustainable Forestry Initiative certification for its recycled papers. Malloy stopped sending waste to landfills in 2009 and uses only soy-, vegetable-, and water-based inks that are free of volatile organic compounds.

Berrett–Koehler
Publishers

Berrett-Koehler is an independent publisher dedicated to an ambitious mission: *Creating a World That Works for All*.

We believe that to truly create a better world, action is needed at all levels—individual, organizational, and societal. At the individual level, our publications help people align their lives with their values and with their aspirations for a better world. At the organizational level, our publications promote progressive leadership and management practices, socially responsible approaches to business, and humane and effective organizations. At the societal level, our publications advance social and economic justice, shared prosperity, sustainability, and new solutions to national and global issues.

A major theme of our publications is "Opening Up New Space." Berrett-Koehler titles challenge conventional thinking, introduce new ideas, and foster positive change. Their common quest is changing the underlying beliefs, mindsets, institutions, and structures that keep generating the same cycles of problems, no matter who our leaders are or what improvement programs we adopt.

We strive to practice what we preach—to operate our publishing company in line with the ideas in our books. At the core of our approach is stewardship, which we define as a deep sense of responsibility to administer the company for the benefit of all of our "stakeholder" groups: authors, customers, employees, investors, service providers, and the communities and environment around us.

We are grateful to the thousands of readers, authors, and other friends of the company who consider themselves to be part of the "BK Community." We hope that you, too, will join us in our mission.

A BK Business Book

This book is part of our BK Business series. BK Business titles pioneer new and progressive leadership and management practices in all types of public, private, and nonprofit organizations. They promote socially responsible approaches to business, innovative organizational change methods, and more humane and effective organizations.

Berrett–Koehler
Publishers

A community dedicated to creating
a world that works for all

Visit Our Website: www.bkconnection.com

Read book excerpts, see author videos and Internet movies, read
our authors' blogs, join discussion groups, download book apps, find
out about the BK Affiliate Network, browse subject-area libraries of
books, get special discounts, and more!

Subscribe to Our Free E-Newsletter, the *BK Communiqué*

Be the first to hear about new publications, special discount offers,
exclusive articles, news about bestsellers, and more! Get on the list
for our free e-newsletter by going to **www.bkconnection.com**.

Get Quantity Discounts

Berrett-Koehler books are available at quantity discounts for orders
of ten or more copies. Please call us toll-free at (800) 929-2929 or
email us at bkp.orders@aidcvt.com.

Join the BK Community

BKcommunity.com is a virtual meeting place where people from
around the world can engage with kindred spirits to create a world
that works for all. **BKcommunity.com** members may create their own
profiles, blog, start and participate in forums and discussion groups,
post photos and videos, answer surveys, announce and register for
upcoming events, and chat with others online in real time. Please join
the conversation!